THIS BOOK IS FOR YOU IF...

- you want to fast-track your success.

- you want to dramatically increase the visibility of your business.

- you want to know what kinds of PR really work in today's marketplace.

- you want to understand the sectrets to effective PR.

- you want to be inspired by other businesses who have achieved success.

- you are open to learning simple marketing strategies that can make all the difference.

- you need to get clarity on your brand.

- you need practical strategies to move your business forward.

WHAT PEOPLE ARE SAYING ABOUT JANEY

"Janey helps you fill in the gaps of the where, how, and who questions, allowing you to get clear about your brand."

Sophia Kupse – www.themusclewhisperer.co.uk

"If you're on a tight budget and need to raise brand awareness, Janey is probably your best bet!"

Nic White – Director, alva UK

"With a gentle touch and easy brilliance, Janey Lee Grace showed me exactly where I need to focus to take my business to the next level."

Shann Jones – Chuckling Goat

"Her huge experience in both the media and the holistic industry helped me to get clear on what makes me unique and the key things to focus on to get the most relevant attention for my business."

Karen Gilbert – The Fragrant Alchemist, www.karengilbert.co.uk

"Her knowledge and first-hand experience of PR and marketing is outstanding. Janey is knowledgeable, highly professional, genuine, down-to-earth and most definitely recommended."

Stephen Pauley – Founder, Be First Class Limited

"My One-to-One Coaching with Janey showed me all the tricks of the trade in my quest to become Radio and TV's favourite Legal Expert."

Mark Betteridge – Betteridge and Co. Solicitors

"Janey's depth of experience from both sides of the PR fence means that she provides a great space for creative dreaming, backed up with the practical solutions to make the dream a reality.

"No matter who you are or what you do, it is always of value to have another point of view, and Janey gave me the opportunity to see my work from another perspective. This supports new opportunities and gave me the chance to focus in a new way."

Jules Wyman – Confidence Coach

"Sparkling! That's the best way to describe how I'm feeling after working with Janey Lee Grace. Sparkling with hope, ideas, gratitude and excitement for the brilliant business vision that has emerged from her questions and insights. Janey teased out the tangled threads inside my head and made a golden ballgown with them...all in under an hour! She really is a fairy godmother. And I shall go to the ball."

Andrea Gardner – CEO Purplefeather Ltd.
Author of 'Change Your Words, Change Your World'

"Janey totally gets how being a holistic practitioner, we have different needs to mainstream businesses, and the small investment I made gave me such content-rich secrets and showed me every step of the way how to raise my profile, stand out from the crowd through building a successful platform, and take my business to the next level. I recommend anyone serious about building their holistic business to make this small investment in themselves and their business to bring lifelong success."

Wendy Fry – Emotional Health; Relationships Consultant,
Author of 'Find YOU, Find LOVE'

*To be successful,
you have to have your heart
in your business,
and your business
in your heart.*

Thomas Watson Senior

ABOUT THE AUTHOR

JANEY LEE GRACE

Janey learned all the tips and secrets that she is offering you today the hard way, but her efforts have rewarded her with, as an author, an Amazon No 1 bestselling book, many national TV appearances as an expert commentator, and, as a presenter, 15 years (and still counting) as a co-presenter on the UK's biggest radio show on BBC Radio 2 (now eight million listeners), and also being voted the No 1 personality in the *Natural Beauty Yearbook* for two years running, as well as a website that received a quarter of a million hits in its first month online. Janey currently write columns for many magazines, and her dedicated PR efforts for individual clients have resulted (for them) in some life-changing media breakthroughs.

But it's not just PR that you need, and sometimes it's finding that clarity and vision that you know is within yourself, and searching for release! Janey wants to help you find that vision, package it, and send it out into the world in a way that will make it listen!

YOU
are the
BRAND

PR secrets to fast-track your visibility and sky-rocket your success

An Introduction to PR / Marketing / Media skills featuring exercises, visualisations, success stories and top tips from inspired authors, experts and business owners.

Janey Lee Grace

Published by
Filament Publishing Ltd
16, Croydon Road, Waddon, Croydon
Surrey CR0 4PA, United Kingdom
Telephone +44(0)20 8688 2598
www.filamentpublishing.com

ISBN 978-1-910819-43-2

Printed by IngramSpark

TABLE OF CONTENTS

Success is about liking yourself,
liking what you do
and liking how to do it.

Maya Angelou

INTRODUCTION

I remember when I held my own first book, *Imperfectly Natural Woman*, in my hand for the first time, hot off the press from a small publisher in Wales, Crown House Publishing. The feeling was second only to giving birth. I felt so proud of my creation; I'd worked SO hard to create this product because I was passionate about my subject and wanted to share my message with the wider world. No one had warned me that just because you release a book or develop and produce a wonderful product, it doesn't mean it gets it 'out there'!

I naively went along to the local bookshop (you can tell that was a few years ago!) to see the display of the brand new book by Janey Lee Grace, only to be told they'd never heard of me and weren't stocking it. Neither were any of the other shops. Around the same time, one of my girlfriends had developed her own awesome natural and organic skincare range literally at her kitchen table. She'd used her savings to invest in great packaging, design and manufacture, as well as a new website and online store. She then waited patiently for orders to fly in but nothing much happened.

We both lamented the miserable, bare truth — unless you are already famous or notorious, your book/product/service/profile will not be a success without good PR and marketing.

I was determined not to let my 'life's work' disappear into the abyss, and so I set about finding a way to promote it. I was lucky enough to get onto a mainstream radio show and had the opportunity to discuss the ideas in my book over the course of an hour with a 'sympathetic' presenter. The book shot to Number 1 on Amazon overnight (knocking *The Da Vinci Code* off the top spot!) and suddenly all those bookshops that had no idea who I was ordered in so many copies that the book instantly sold out and we were onto our second print run. My girlfriend, the aforementioned one whose organic skincare range was promoted in the book and on the radio show, (we'd talked about it in the interview) also found her business catapulted to success, and it's going from strength to strength!

Of course, it may not happen that way for you, and you may not wish to write a book, but the basic principles apply. If you have a passion and a purpose, a product you have created, a message that you want to share; whether you are an author, an expert, a small business owner, therapist, teacher or artisan producer; this book is for you. Why learn from me? Because I have combined my twenty-five years of experience in the media as a producer, journalist, presenter and interviewer with my nine years of being 'on the other side of the fence' as an author/businesswoman trying to get noticed and sustain a profitable business working with my passion and purpose.

Hopefully you were attracted to this book because you want to get your business and brand more visibility, and you want to work and create SUCCESS with your passion.

This is not a business course. I won't cover time management, accounting or spreadsheets, but I aim to help you to 'fast-track' DIY ways for you to get the kind of PR exposure, visibility and credibility you deserve to put yourself and your business on the map, without paying fortunes to PR companies! You can do it on your own, and I'm going to show you how – I want to give you some pointers, all the tricks and tips to help get YOU out there. I would suggest a rough framework of six weeks to complete these steps; technically you could complete them sooner but given that most of us are time-poor, six weeks feels like a good amount of time to commit to a PR/marketing strategy that will stand you in good stead for anything you want to promote, both now and in the future. There are five steps to complete but some will take longer than others, and there are some valuable exercises – again, some will take longer than others but they can be mostly used immediately on your website so no time is wasted!

I've also included some 'success stories' of people who have taken the step, done their own PR and got themselves into the spotlight. I'm not necessarily talking about entrepreneurs who have made their millions, as reading those kinds of success stories sometimes feel too separate from our own lives. I'm going to showcase 'ordinary' people (except that no one is ordinary – everyone is special!), who have started with a passion and been able to authentically grow or promote their business and build that all-important platform. While they may have not necessarily made their millions yet, they are well on the way to feeling fulfilled with the opportunities they have managed to attract, and importantly they have maximised those opportunities admirably. Don't underestimate the power of good media relations... in the words of some of the Great and the Good...

*It is not enough that a man
has clearness of vision,
and reliance on sincerity,
he must also have the
art of expression,
or he will remain obscure.*

George H. Lewes

PR FOR YOU AND YOUR BRAND

Publicity is absolutely critical.
A good PR story is infinitely
more effective than a front page ad

Sir Richard Branson

Why is PR and/or media coverage so important for individuals, experts, authors and small businesses?

PR is Public Relations. It's about your relationship with potential clients and people in the media who can help get your message out there. Despite our best hopes though, it doesn't always come easily. Effort and tenacity are required!

If you're thinking, "Surely it's enough just to be good at what I do, and then clients and consumers will come and buy?" Yes, some might! You may be already very busy with clients or have a thriving business, but you know that you have so much more to share to a far wider audience. That's why you're attracted to this book.

My guess is that even if you are happy with your success or your client list, you still have a message of some kind that you really want to get out there to a wider audience, whether in the form of a book, TV/radio, online programmes, events, apps or workshops. Whatever form it comes in, it's BIG and it's a burning desire within you.

If that resonates, I'd go so far as to say it's your DUTY to get that message out there!

Marianne Williamson, author of *The Age of Miracles*, said, *"We are all born carrying a promise – a promise to make the world better – and there's a yearning to make good on that promise that none of us can suppress forever."*

Let's establish one important principle: it's important for you to see that you are a brand in order to be able to become more visible in terms of PR and marketing. This doesn't compromise on any of your authenticity; it's simply a way to enable people to know that they have found the right person, the right company for them. If you have a strong brand promise and people know what you stand for, then you will attract the right people for you, those that you can help.

You need to put the 'You' back into your business. We all know about the importance of the Unique Selling Point – the USP; it could also be called your PSP – Personality Selling Proposition! Even if you don't yet have a business, it's still worth considering 'Personal Branding'. Really be aware of what you are a 'stand for': what are your unique qualities, gifts and talents, your 'point of difference'? Ask yourself what is your clear vision and purpose for your future (whether personal or business).

How you 'PR' and 'market' your personal and professional brand is key. Your reputation is at stake, and by really having clarity on exactly who you are and what your clear vision is, you can take back control over your potential success...

Bill Gates famously once said, *"If I had one dollar left, I'd spend it on marketing."*

Now you may immediately think, "But he's all 'corporate'! I'm just me in my therapy room treating clients or in my workshop making laundry products, or hiring IT people to run a busy online store." Well, even if you feel you have enough clients to treat right now, or you have enough people buying your products to tick over, what about all that knowledge and inspiration that you have that you could share? If you were willing to think outside the box, you could get YOUR message out to a wider audience. I often find myself working with people whose passion and purpose is to educate or help others, who went into business in order to help people. If that's you, recognise that you will help far more people if you reach out; the 'It all' starts with people like you getting their message out there.

There may be a part of you thinking anything to do with public relations is a bit sleazy, that it's for the likes of politicians and spin doctors to feed us the lines they want us to hear, and often is just there as a means to cover up what's really going on!

Certainly, PR can have a bad rap and can get associated with backbiting ruthless corporate firms, but if it's AUTHENTIC, it can also be a wonderful way of spreading information about a product or service that can bring great benefit to a wide number of people.

Good public relations, especially for small businesses and individuals operating as sole traders, is primarily about connecting with the right audience and conveying the benefits that you could bring to them.

If you are working with your passion and you genuinely want to make a difference, I hope you recognise that you are part of a new kind of consciousness; the more people who know about your product or service, the more successful you will be, and the more people you can serve.

> *Brand is not a product,*
> *that's for sure;*
> *it's not one item.*
> *It's an idea, it's a theory,*
> *it's a meaning,*
> *it's how you carry yourself.*
> *It's aspirational,*
> *it's inspirational.*
>
> **Kevin Plank**

YOU ARE THE BRAND - YOUR YOU-SP (USP)

So if we have established that it's about real, authentic people connecting with a potential audience, let's look at this concept of You as the brand. This can be the stumbling block for many professionals, and yet it's absolutely key to your moving forward and to your success. For example, therapists, especially if they use a recognised discipline such as reflexology, will often say, "Oh, it's not about me, it's reflexology that's great!"

That's true, but there are many reflexologists and only one YOU! If you are looking to attract more clients and widen your opportunities for your knowledge and passion, then you need to market and promote your particular USP – your Unique Selling Point or Unique Selling Proposition.

Ask.com defines USP as: *The Unique Selling Point (or Unique Selling Proposition) is a marketing concept that was initially proposed as a theory to give an explanation. This is to a pattern among advertising campaigns of the early 1940s that were successful. It states that such campaigns made unique propositions to the consumers convincing them to switch brands.*

So let's look at what that really means – what is it that sets you apart? Why is it so crucial to be clear on your USP? Your YOU-SP?

I'm sure you've heard the saying – people do business with those they like, know and trust. Think about that within your own life; do you have a favourite hairdresser? Are you equally happy to go to any stylist in that salon? Usually not! If you have regular massages, do you go to a different masseur each time? Are you confident to go to any dentist in any town? It's unlikely. Technically, of course, any hairdresser or dentist ought to suit your needs; it's likely they will all have some prerequisites – in the case of a hairdresser, some good scissors, hairdryer and straighteners, and, in the case of a dentist, the right high-tech dentistry tools...but, of course, it's about SO much more than that.

I've recently found a wonderful therapist who lives close to me. She understands my needs, she's not afraid to tell me off when I'm not scheduling enough 'me time' and I really feel the benefit from a treatment with her and from her considerable experience and knowledge. I really like her; it's not just the therapeutic treatment.

From a business perspective, I'm her ideal client. I'll keep going back to her because I like, know and trust her. Interestingly, it's getting harder and harder to get an appointment because I also recommend her to just about everyone else and many people have started going to her – that's the power of the testimonial!

WHY IS IT IMPORTANT THAT YOU ESTABLISH YOURSELF AS THE BRAND?

Let's say it again – because people do business with those they like, know and trust. In order for us to get to know the person who is the face of the brand, they need to be visible. Many successful brands are 'personality led'. Even the big corporate companies know this, which is why we all think of Richard Branson as soon as we hear the name Virgin Atlantic, we remember that Jamie Oliver was the public face of Sainsbury's, while the late Dame Anita Roddick was very much the face and public persona of her brand, The Body Shop. One of the originals from the TV show *Dragons' Den*, Theo Paphitis, is very visible within the brands he owns. You'll see big full-length pictures of him in the front windows of many Ryman stores. It gives the brand a connection with a REAL PERSON.

There are many 'personal brands' that have strong associations. If we think about celebrity chefs, we immediately think of Nigella Lawson and Jamie Oliver. If we are discussing football, it's unlikely we will get through a sentence without mentioning David Beckham. 'YouTubers' are the new pop stars of their generation; my kids are great fans of vloggers such as Alfie, Zoella and Marcus Butler; these were just 'regular' young people who started out making videos or 'vlogs' which, because they developed a certain style, appealed to a huge number of people. They started to attract hundreds of thousands of views and, in recent years, have been able to monetise this in association with YouTube, been able to negotiate huge sponsorship deals and have joined the breed of new successful entrepreneurs though establishing their strong personal brand. It's been critically important for them to recognise their individuality, their You-SP and their YOU-nique brilliance.

"But that's not me," I can almost hear you shouting, "I'm not a high-flying businesswoman like Anita Roddick or a multimillion selling author and entrepreneur like Jamie!" Maybe that's true, but if you have a product that people want to buy or a service that people need, then you are providing a solution for a problem that certain people have. As a result, it will be much easier to get your message out to those people, and to let them know it's you or your products that they need. If there is a clear brand identity, a core brand message and USP, a real person that the potential buyer can connect with, someone who seems like an OK person who seems trustworthy, who seems in some ways just like them; someone they could like, know, and trust, it will be even easier to make connections. Getting clarity on your personal brand will help you to set your business goals, to define your purpose, and it will help you to know exactly who your target clients or audience are and how best you can communicate with them and become the perfect 'brand' for them.

To establish yourself as the brand, we have to get to see you. You need to be visible – putting yourself in the spotlight is going to be important for you, for the benefit of your business and from an altruistic perspective for the good of us all, because you have such great information to share. If modesty is your thing and confidence is an issue, you may want to hide away rather than stand in the spotlight – it's like that for very many sole traders, entrepreneurs and professionals. Perhaps you switched from a lucrative career and retrained, so somehow it doesn't feel right to even be discussing business growth and expansion, let alone the tricky topic of money and what you charge for what you do. I really want to urge you to put modesty aside and remember that the smaller you keep your business, the less people you can help. It sounds obvious, but it's true. Feeling fully confident to stand in your spotlight is of such huge importance and I have found that it's one of the most popular topics in my courses and trainings in this subject. We all know that the cockiest most outgoing person can fall to pieces when asked to speak in public or be interviewed; we've had great authentic authors in at the radio station who managed to blow a golden opportunity to speak to eight million people! Usually it comes down to confidence and preparation...

If you aren't naturally a Jamie Oliver, how do you gain confidence to stand in the spotlight, whether that's to speak at a networking event, attend a 'meet the buyer' event, record a YouTube video, or be interviewed on the radio?

This is the important tip here...it's all about Preparation. There's more to come on this, but trust me, feeling fully prepared will help you to deliver.

It's important to remember that it's rather like 'acting work'; I don't mean you are acting the role of someone completely different, but you are indeed 'acting' as your highest, most confident, energetic self. I want you to learn how to be fully prepared so that you can literally EMBODY your message.

There are wonderful techniques and resources that can help with this; if you can overcome any cynicism, then it's worth remembering that the power of the subconscious mind cannot be overestimated. There are aspects of NLP (Neurolinguistic Programming), TFT (Thought Field Therapy) and EFT (Emotional Freedom Technique) which really work to help with focusing ourselves and feeling confident in a situation where you could feel nervous to the point of it being debilitating and hampering your performance.

You need to feel confident to stand in the spotlight, so that you become the 'go-to' expert – the confident 'media-friendly' commentator that producers and editors want to feature.

Your 'brand message', i.e. your USP, must be there throughout, and a core part of your brand message is you. It can feel a little scary, a bit like taking your clothes off in public, but it is necessary to share aspects of your personality with your ideal clients in order to establish your brand. By that, I don't mean your clients need to delve into the skeletons in your closet; you can choose the aspects of yourself and your story that you wish to share, but I will encourage you to look at which are the most beneficial.

When you are clear on your brand and your message and how you see your vision and purpose for your work, it becomes easier to see how you can start to establish yourself as the expert that everyone wants to work with.

CAN PR HELP ME REACH MY IDEAL CLIENTS?

I f we accept that PR is important, let's ask, how will you use PR and marketing to get to your ideal clients?

Throughout this book, we will look at some of the many different ways you can get your message out, be visible, and really create and maximise opportunities for your business within the wider media, and also in order to attract paying clients.

I'm sure you are well aware that when it comes to brand marketing, there a different ways of targeting your ideal clients. One method is by blanket advertising; i.e. placing expensive ads across a wide range of publications or even advertising hoardings, as a rule, I believe generic advertising alone rarely works for small businesses or for individuals. It's usually far too general, difficult to quantify, very expensive and can yield zero results. What's usually far more effective is to target your ideal clients and try and forge connections with potential target clients. This is kind of obvious; I'm sure few of you would consider paying thousands of pounds for an advert in the back of a national newspaper when you could place a small ad against some editorial in a local publication aimed at people interested in your specific business.

It's obvious you would want to place advertisements where people interested in what you sell might go, but you'd be amazed how many small businesses and entrepreneurs are lured into paying a small fortune for an advert in a mainstream publication, only to feel bitterly let down (and financially stretched) when it yields little or no results. One client of mine had a fitness brand and spent thousands of pounds placing a poster outside an underground station in central London; they were convinced that health-conscious passers-bys would flock to their fitness studio just a hundred yards from the station. The result? Zero new clients. They would have been far better to offer a free membership/fitness sessions to a journalist or columnist writing for a health and well-being/fitness magazine and get a favourable editorial piece read by their direct target market.

> ## *Love what you do.*
> ## *Do what you love.*
>
> **Wayne Dyer**

WHO ARE YOUR IDEAL CLIENTS?

Let's look at niching down even further before you make any plans for ads, editorials, or indeed any kind of marketing. First of all, be absolutely clear on who is your ideal client and look to building your target group, 'your tribe' as it is sometimes called. Now, this can be another sticking point for some sole traders – so often, you are so sure that you can help everyone, that you can end up helping very few! On one of my individual coaching calls, I asked a massage therapist what her speciality was. She said, "Everything. I can help people with any ailments whatsoever." I asked her who was her ideal client. "Everyone," she said. "All ages, both sexes – everyone." I asked what she had been doing to attract new clients as she was not busy with a full client list and she said, "Leaving piles of brochures in the local Indian restaurant." They were brochures that contained a huge list of ailments and how her treatments might help, in the hope that if someone would pick it up, it would resonate with their particular health condition and they would book an appointment.

Not surprisingly, she had received not one new enquiry as a result of her marketing. Why? Because trying to attract everyone equals attracting no one!

So how do we identify our ideal clients and get our message out to them?

Let's start with the defining; how do we tap into the kind of people who want and need our services? It's a great idea to really spend some time visualising your ideal client. This is sometimes called your client 'Avatar' – a fictional character but someone who represents your ideal client. It really helps to create the story connected to your client avatar; it could help you with some key insights.

It may be someone you know, someone who is already a client, or someone you can imagine in great detail. Put yourself in their shoes and think what is that they need that you can offer. When you've identified your ideal client, it's so much easier to then target your PR and market to them; if you offer a service in a local area, then it's OK to leave some leaflets and brochures where you know your ideal clients hang out, but the important thing is to identify other ways that you can connect with the wider audience, the potential ideal 'tribe'.

RESISTANCE?

There's often resistance to this, as, just like the therapist I mentioned, many people from a very altruistic perspective genuinely believe that everyone is a client for them, that they really don't need to niche down. The belief is, 'If I build it, they will all come' – let's hope so, but let's get the right people for you coming along who will in turn recommend you to the right people.

I heard a wonderful analogy once – Corrina Gordon-Barnes speaks of the importance of finding your niche and your tribe; she likens anyone working with their passion as a sort of guardian angel. It's a lovely thought – imagine yourself with your wings spread wide around your tribe, the people who really need you to look after them; you are their guardian angel and they are your ideal clients. If you imagine looking around in 'holistic heaven', you can see other guardian angels with their tribes too. Now imagine that you had decided you simply must be the answer to everyone's needs; you could flit about flapping your wings and try and drip a bit of help here, and a feather of hope there, but ultimately in trying to be all things to everyone, you may end up serving no one. Really try and get in touch with who you are the guardian angel for!

Of course, if you become a bestselling author, or hugely successful brand, you could be touching the lives of millions, and you will need a much bigger wingspan then. However, if you are at a part of your business or career journey where you're still getting established, becoming known or are in the process of growing a client list, it's a brilliant idea to choose an aspect of your business, find the niche that you can serve, and keep them in mind as your client when you plan your strategy for PR and marketing. Remember, this is a real person you are connecting with.

If this is a new concept for you, you will need to spend some time on this. It's really worth compiling a list of different groups of people that could be your ideal tribes, and then perhaps narrow that down to just one group. By really having clarity on your ideal client profile, you will have a better idea where you should be concentrating your efforts PR-wise, and what kind of copy you should use to attract them, as well as what elements of your story will be most of interest to them.

Give them a name and visualise them in detail. Some people even create a fictional client avatar using an online avatar building programme. Create a kind of CV for them. Where do they work? Are they married, or single? Do they have children? Any hobbies? Some elements will be more relevant than others. Importantly, ask yourself what is their story; what is it that they need? What are they looking for when they find your product or service, and how might they be thinking about it?

As service providers, it's often easy to forget about the journey the customer goes through when they buy from us, so it's really worth putting yourself in the shoes of this ideal client, become your client avatar, search your product, and see how the customer feels with the ease of use, with the connection, etc. Can they find out about your product easily? Can they instantly like, know and trust you? Sometimes by defining your ideal client and putting yourself literally in their thoughts, you may discover a better way of serving them, or you may come up with a clearer idea of the content they would like to read, or the special offer that might appeal most.

Let's suppose you work as an organic skincare specialist. One of your target groups could be women concerned about ageing. Write down what you know those women are looking for, the problems they might put into Google or other search engines – 'anti-ageing naturally' or 'Is there a natural Botox?', for example. Perhaps your avatar is indeed a woman who wants to look good but doesn't want to go down the route of invasive cosmetic surgery. These words and phrases can become your keywords, so it's worth spending some time on getting them right. Ask yourself, 'What problem does my ideal client have that I can provide a solution for?' Take yourself through the thought process of that client and ask yourself whether the last blog post you wrote, or the last piece of content you uploaded to a social networking site, might be of interest to them. If so, what's next? Can you invite them to sign up to receive your video series on natural anti-ageing, or is there a special discount on skincare? Hopefully, you can feel much more connection with what your ideal client wants when you know where they are coming from.

Don't fall into the trap of merely recognising what you are good at teaching and hoping people will be searching for that. For example, one of my clients is a woman's life coach. I asked her about her specific niche, what her point of difference was. Her reply was, "I am a transformer." Now, of course, I know that she means she can facilitate transformation for women, but I had an immediate vision of a robotic toy! I helped her realise that her ideal clients won't be searching for help with 'transformation' – they may not have such a word on their radar at all – it's far more likely that they will be searching for 'feel less stressed', 'overwhelm', or 'better relationships'.

By really identifying what your ideal client needs that you can help them with, you can use those phrases in your copy in order to attract them to you. You can then find ways to connect to him or her and show that you have an understanding of their needs and that you can help. Of course, some people merely want to put their credit card into an online store and buy a pot of cream that promises to take away their wrinkles, or are prepared to take a punt on an online course to help them reduce their stress, but a growing number of people want to go deeper and find someone who really seems to understand where their particular needs lie.

If they can 'connect with 'You', and at first glance at least feel they could like or trust you, then that's much less clinical. Now they are buying into an emotion and that's far more powerful and far more likely to turn them into a client. That's why good PR is about you standing strong in your authenticity, being really clear about what you represent, and being willing to connect with those for whom you can provide the solution for their problem.

*Communication is a skill
that you can learn.
It's like riding a bicycle or typing.
If you're willing to work at it,
you can rapidly improve the
quality of every part of your life.*

Brian Tracy

YOU AS THE GO-TO EXPERT

It's important to be clear as to exactly how to approach journalists and producers and try to ensure that you are ready if you were to be called in as the expert. But how do you establish yourself as the 'go-to' expert in your field? One of the great ways is to write a book. I highly recommend everyone thinks about it. If you have a message to get out there, it doesn't have to be *War and Peace*, a short eBook would do it, twenty-five pages!

When you have written a book, it's a calling card, you are an author – <u>add three letters and you are an Authority</u>. It's one sure-fire way of attracting journalists and producers. When we look for experts to interview on national radio, the first ones that we'll go for are the authors.

It's important to be clear on what you should prepare in advance if you are contacting journalists, how to come up with different angles for new stories that come up again and again, and how to respond to current stories. Let's look at an example of how that might work.

Let's say you are an EFT practitioner specialising in treating phobias, amongst other things. You live in a small town or village and have a client list that sometimes refers you to others.

Let's suppose there was a news story hitting the headlines, perhaps a celeb or someone in the public eye admitted to a phobia of flying. Sometimes, these kinds of stories run and run. You may be watching the local breakfast TV news in your area or listening to national radio hearing doctors and various psychology experts talking about the fear of flying and you'll be screaming at the TV, "I can cure that easily!" Well don't wait for someone else more savvy to call up the station or email the newspaper, you do it! In fact, in an ideal world, you would have already made yourself known to journalists and producers, especially locally.

If you had written a short eBook on how to deal with phobias naturally, then that would give you the perfect 'credentials' to approach them and offer yourself as a commentator.

It's important to look at how you get your message out to journalists and to potential clients through education-based marketing for your brand. That means creating and sharing content – writing articles and blogs, perhaps writing a book, whether that be a self-published eBook or a physical book, running teleseminar courses, recording podcasts or YouTube videos, the list is endless. By education-based marketing, I mean you are helping to educate others about what it is you know about that could benefit them. It all helps to big up you and your brand.

I hope you can see how this exposure, just by linking to a current news story, could massively benefit you and establish your brand as an authentic authority.

QUICK SUMMARY

1. **If you're Authentic, PR is not a dirty word.** Remember the more successful you are, the more your work is making the world a better place.

2. **You are the brand**, your business is all about you, and by telling your story and being clear on your USP, you can see how you can relate to your ideal clients and to your niche tribe. So you need to get in touch with all the 'best bits of you' and your product or service, and know what your USP is.

3. **People do business with those that they like, know, and trust** – and this is the reason you must put yourself at the head of your brand.

4. **Harness the confident outgoing part of you in order to be able to stand in your spotlight.** Look into EFT and TFT and see if you can begin to imagine yourself feeling very confident to share your own story. Imagine yourself in the spotlight standing with confidence and see yourself as the person your ideal clients will like, know and trust.

5. **Identify one person that is your ideal client** – they can be real or imaginary – and ask yourself every time you write a blog, article, press release or plan any action, "What would my ideal client think?"

One of the training courses I run is called **Supercharge BOTH sides of your brand**.

It's hugely important to recognise the 360 degree picture of your brand, the whole. If you see it as two semicircles connecting (with YOU in the middle of the circle, 'You are the brand!'), then look at the two halves. On one side, you want to attract and sell to your ideal clients and customers; if you are an author, blogger or expert, you will want to increase your community or your tribe. On the other side, you want to attract and maximise PR and media attention, raise your profile, and become the Go-to expert in your field.

To sell to clients and increase community...

Blogging regularly, Operate an Effective Sales Funnel, Be Active on Social Media, Showcase at Exhibitions/Events....

To attract PR and Media Attention

Be 'PR-ready' with a Press Kit, Be a great Public Speaker, Have written a book or other newsworthy content, have audio and visual examples of yourself in action.

There may be as many as ten different ways you are attracting both, but what I commonly find is that people are far stronger in one area than the other – many small business owners are very savvy with their sales techniques and marketing, but when it comes to PR and marketing, they don't even have a decent high resolution image of their product, let alone themselves! On the other hand, there are authors and speakers who regularly speak at events, write columns and often get featured as an expert commentator, but have nothing to upsell from their media exposure (other than perhaps their book).

Recognise that both sides of your brand need to be coherent and creative. For the purpose of this exercise, use the diagram below or create your own, and come up with at least five actions you are currently taking to connect with your clients and five actions you are taking to attract media and PR – of course, there may be overlap but you should be including such ideas as...

Website
Sales Funnel

Press Pack

Have absolute clarity on your Brand Definition and ask yourself how you want to be defined and recognised by both your clients and the media. What do you want to be known for, and who do you represent? How you choose to communicate your brand values will have a direct impact on the customers and clients and the media attention that you attract. Make sure there is a synergy – people buy into your authentic story and your strong brand identity. Similarly, journalists, editors and producers want to give you column inches or airtime because their readers and listeners will identify with your key messages.

*If a brand genuinely
wants to make a
social contribution,
it should start with
who they are,
not what they do.
For only when a brand has
defined itself and
its core values can it identify
causes or social responsibility
initiatives that are in alignment
with its authentic brand story.*

Simon Mainwaring

THE FIVE STEPS TO BRAND YOU

Once you have grasped that you need real clarity on your You-nique brilliance and your USP, here my top five strategies in detail for getting the visibility that You and Your Brand deserve.

STEP 1
CREATE COMPELLING CONTENT

Copy, articles, e-zines, press releases, even your own website text, is how the world can get to hear about you. Leave them wanting more! It's imperative to tap into the ways your written words can grab the attention of your clients, future clients, and the media. There are a whole myriad of resources, tips, tools and techniques on my audio courses and even freely available that can help you create compelling content. It could be time to find the confidence to write that book you've always dreamed of writing; they do say there's a book in all of us, but if for you the dream has just felt too overwhelming, think again – you don't have to write *War and Peace*, you could write a short eBook. If you think you aren't a natural writer, I'd urge you to let go of that; I wasn't ever a literary pro (still aren't!), but I am passionate about sharing the information and knowledge I have and there's authenticity in that. Don't forget you can always get someone to edit your work; a good editor will still keep your 'voice' so that it sounds authentic.

If you are fearful you won't attract a publisher, again that's not an excuse anymore, as many very successful authors choose to self-publish; in fact, right now you're reading a self-published book from a No 1 bestselling author! It's now perfectly acceptable. One author colleague of mine recently turned down a very lucrative offer from a mainstream publisher because she wanted to keep control and a larger percentage of the profits. It's important to remember that a potential client (your ideal client) may not want to spend hours on your website, or indeed reading your press releases, but if you genuinely have some knowledge to share, they may well be interested to read it in order to be 'educated', so if they have that on their Kindle or e-reader, or in paperback form, as they head onto the train or the beach, they will be willing to invest in that. From the point of view of attracting media attention, many doors open when you become an author. A book is not often a money-spinner except for the lucky few, but it is an excellent calling card. Remember, once you add three letters to the word Author – you become an 'Author-ity'.

Producers and editors may well call you for comment because you are an author. By sharing your knowledge, you share something of yourself and your enthusiasm – that in turn attracts people to you and to your brand, because, here's that phrase again, 'People do business with those they like, know and trust'. Don't underestimate the power of a book to get your message out there. Of course, not everyone who reads your book will become a client (if they did, I'd be very happy – albeit overwhelmed) but many will, or they could pass on the info to others who might, or indeed they may just be helped or inspired by your words – how fulfilling is that?

If you're already an author, how do you get the world to know about your book? I think most people realise that writing a book, even if it's published with a well-known publishing house, doesn't mean it will hit the bookshelves. There is, however, lots you can do yourselves. Find as many opportunities as possible to get your book reviewed and use your own content in bite-size nuggets for social networking. It's hugely important to establish yourself as an authority in people's eyes; make sure that they know you are the 'go-to' expert. It's much easier once you have a published book, become known for a blog, or even become adept at promoting your articles on social networking, to use the tricks to grab the attention of journalists, producers and buyers. It's worth bearing in mind though that anyone in the media is time-poor and with a different agenda to yours; they simply don't care if you have a great new product or have opened up a juice bar – unless you catch their eye with a press release or similar that offers a great angle (remember that journalists and editors need to fill column inches and radio producers need to fill airtime). All of them are crying out for relevant content that their target audience will find interesting.

It's imperative, therefore, to write inspiring, compelling copy that 'sings' to its reader!

It's worth remembering that not everyone is your ideal client, but here are some interesting statistics. It's generally considered in marketing terms that at any given time:

- 30 per cent of people are not interested at all in your offer,
- 30 per cent are not even conscious that they might need you, not aware of their problem,
- 30 per cent are aware that they could need you at some point,
- 7 per cent are open to what you are offering, and
- ONLY 3 per cent are actively looking for it.

Now, when we think of sales and marketing, we tend to think of hard sales, like car sales, or perhaps double glazing or new windows. Those people are aiming their marketing at the three per cent who are actively looking to replace a car or windows, and the brand want to be the one that's chosen. That's exactly right, of course, because unless you are thinking about buying a new car, it's totally irrelevant to you whether Saab or Mitsubishi are doing deals or promotions!

But with your brand, business or service, which hopefully either solves a problem for people or makes them feel good, you can focus on education-based marketing which could easily convert the three per cent who are already looking for YOU, but could also connect with the seven per cent that are open and possibly convert them to sales.

Your content could connect with the 30 per cent that are aware that they may need you at some point and the 30 per cent not yet conscious that they may need you. This is education-based marketing; it's exactly that, educating people – reminding them or teaching them something they didn't know before.

So how do you start to make a connection with those people? First, to state the obvious, you need a good product or service; it needs to be great ingredients, the right packaging or a strong brand promise and USP, but let's assume that's in place. As you know, this book is about how to get your business visible, so let's assume you are clear on your USP and you know what it is you want to get out there to that wider audience.

One of the simplest ways to get started in education-based marketing is to write content about the subjects your potential clients are interested in and the benefits you can provide. For example, if you are an Alexander technique practitioner, you could write an educational blog or article about back pain or bad posture, then in the last third of the article, how Alexander technique can help with back problems later (remember, too, you can produce content in other ways, such as audio, video etc.). Don't wait to be asked by a journalist if they can write about you (we will talk more about getting in touch with journalists and producers later), but first get writing yourself to start connecting with those possible percentages who may need your information.

CAN'T WRITE?

Maybe you feel you just can't write. Maybe you were lousy at writing essays at school. Somehow you never could manage to construct even passionate love letters and basically you don't enjoy writing anything more than a to-do list.

THE FIRST THING TO SAY IS STOP PANICKING!

The truth is there are very few people who can't write if they just pick up a <u>few basic skills</u> and reframe the way they think about writing, and ditch the old school day exam mentality!

The first most important thing to remember, whether you are planning a book, some articles, a blog, or even if you just want to write copy for your own website or brochure, is that <u>you do not have to have great literary skills</u>. We are not talking Charles Dickens or even J.K. Rowling, we are simply trying to establish ways for your knowledge, opinions and helpful information to be able to reach a wider audience, and being able to communicate via the written word is a major player in that. There are other tools as well, of course, and we will come onto public speaking and presentations, audio, video promotions etc. but for many, the first port of call is getting your blogs, articles, tips, 'how to' ideas out there and offering content and information, both about yourself and your brand, as a way of connecting with clients and with the media.

Now, I didn't think I could write at all. A publisher came to me and suggested I wrote my first book after hearing me on the radio. I told her I couldn't write and she said, "Well it's not a literary work; it's not as if I'm asking you to write about military history either. You simply have to write what you know. Write from your heart – write how you speak, and if it's really terrible, editors will tidy it up."

I did just that. I wrote *Imperfectly Natural Woman* in a style very similar to how I speak. It became a Amazon Number 1 bestselling book and I've since gone on to write five further books. I am now a regular columnist and a freelance features writer for several magazines and newspapers, and I'm regularly asked to comment and give advice or opinions for other journalists' features. I'm not a literary queen; far from it – I literally write how I speak, I always edit my own work or ask someone else who I trust to look through it. It's really worth several read-throughs to see if I can improve on it, but I'm not talking needing to go to a thesaurus for every word, it's just the odd phrase that comes across better in print if it is presented a different way. I hope that might encourage you; in most cases, if you know your content and you can speak, then you can write ! And if you really can't, well there are other ways to get your content across. You can sublet it out; outsource to a freelance writer – you can get excellent virtual assistants from websites such as Elance and GetFriday, though it's a good idea to ensure that you hire someone who speaks excellent English! If you get busy, it's fine to outsource some articles and blogs, but give writing a shot first, because there could be occasions where you will be required to get the information from out of your head, and onto a page in some form before it can be turned into an article, marketing copy or blog.

SOME GREAT TIPS FOR WRITING CONTENT

- It's not a grammar test – the best writers break all the rules. You do NOT have to be F. Scott Fitzgerald or even J.K. Rowling.

- Don't confuse people with jargon – never use a long word when a short one will do. Write the way people think, and the way you and others speak.

- Edit it down. People are 'time-poor'. Keep it simple; the consumer doesn't have time for complex copy, but deliver your message with clarity.

- Don't forget your brand name (it's amazing the amount of people who do!) and your keywords – remember to include the kind of phrases your clients might be googling / searching for.

- Find, or invent, a creative title, hook, or link to topical, relatable events or current news stories – be 'in the loop'.

CAN GREAT CONTENT TRANSLATE TO SALES?

It's estimated that every day, more than 27 million pieces of content are shared on the Web. It must be working, because statistics show that...

- 61 per cent of marketers use social media to increase lead generation.

- 75 per cent of buyers are likely to use social media in the purchase process.

- 67 per cent more leads per month are generated by companies who blog. That's why for businesses, key influencers are hugely important too. Think of the recent success of blogger turned author Deliciously Ella, and the phenomenon of YouTubers such as Zoella, Alfie, and Marcus Butler

BLOGS

Blogs are brilliant for making you visible on a regular basis. They are much less static than websites, but if you are already feeling exhausted at the thought of daily blogging, be assured you don't need to worry that a blog is a 'diary'; it isn't and it doesn't have to be updated every day, or even every other day. In fact, a blog site can be a holding site for your articles. It's so easy to update regularly, but that doesn't have to mean major adjustments.

So what do you blog about? It's not the same as tweeting or even keeping a diary – don't blog about what you had for breakfast, unless healthy breakfasts are your USP. You can write blog posts on anything that you think people will want to read. Always be willing to offer tips and ideas for free to potentially interested readers; anything titled 'How to...' will always be of interest. Or 'The Top Five ways to...' Don't panic that you will be giving away all your best information for free; just keep your blogs short (maximum 500 words) and, if possible, remember those statistics. Ask yourself, who are you trying to reach with your education-based marketing?

If your potential clients get to know a little bit about you, they feel connected and they will want to access your free gift and sign up to your newsletter or e-zine. That's how you can turn interested parties into clients who will buy from you when the right product is in place for them.

You can make your blog 'date related' by writing about what is affecting you, or how you feel about things that everyone else is talking about.

When you blog, <u>find and react to current news items</u>. Check out what's in the papers and media, and comment on it in your blog. And, a TOP TIP HERE, <u>use the headline in your article</u>. If it's a headline that everyone's *talking* about, they'll be googling it too, so they may just find YOUR article (it has to be relevant to your USP though). This is how you can get these current news trends working for you.

We will be looking later at how you can attract the attention of journalists, but don't wait for journalists or producers to cover a particular topic; you can publish your own take on anything. For example, a good friend of mine, who is an author and nutritionist and diet expert, blogs weekly with a round-up of all the week's major news stories that are linked to food, obesity, weight loss and diet. She gives her unique spin on the current news and, in so doing, she links back to her own books and websites.

Blogs are a great way to link to news stories to begin to set yourself up as an important voice. Whatever is currently in the news that relates to your business, get used to brainstorming all the different angles.

Remember a blog doesn't have to be long; 500 words is fine. It's just your take on something and a call to action to point interested parties to more info. To give a couple of quick examples, when the London Olympics were rocking, I helped out Tiana Fair Trade Products, who make coconut oil and associated products, to create a blog that linked the benefits of using coconut oil as a multifunctional product for athletes, because it helps speed up metabolism, and another to show off that one of the Olympic athletes favoured Tiana Coconut Water to put back electrolytes after his long jump stints. These were blogs, but they were also adapted into press releases which were sent to journalists.

One of the important points to remember for a blog, article or post are that a good headline is essential. If you are linking it to a news story, you can use the same headline as the news story used, though of course, you must credit the source and the journalist etc., and then go on to write your opinion piece. Or, if you are writing a general article, then as already discussed it might be a, 'How to…'or, 'Top Five Tips', or perhaps, '9 benefits of eating raw food' or whatever your subject matter is.

Always include a picture, if appropriate, with your blog article and don't forget that you can then post a message on Facebook and Twitter linking to your blog, including your killer headline which will still be imperative for you.

Make sure there is some kind of call to action and a kickback to you. A blog is not about overt selling, but there's no reason why at the end of your blog you can't point people to sign up to receive your newsletter and to get your free gift.

Make sure you get the tags and description right. If that doesn't mean much to you, you'll need to read up on SEO – search engine optimisation.

Where does the blog 'live' on the web? It's OK to have a blog as part of your site, but it can stand alone too. I prefer that, because the dedicated blog programs like WordPress and Blogger are so good, and there's thousands of people all round the world trying to make them better, simpler, and more fun! I like WordPress because it can look like a website, hold a store etc., (though it is slightly more difficult to set up). Blogger is good too – I have both.

The thing to remember is that Google *likes* blogs, and the 'spiders' will often pick up the subject matter in a blog before they find a website so it can make you visible quickly. You may also attract comments and followers so you can become part of a bloggers' network.

The blogs can then remain on the blog site or on your main website as articles. Remember it's your content so there's no reason why you can't write a short blog post and then encourage people to come over to your website to read the full article there. You can also offer your services as a guest blogger to other websites and online publications where the target audience may be similar to yours.

It's really worth writing blogs, and if you are new to education-based marketing and content writing, it can really work quickly for you. One of my PR and Media Skills Masterclass clients, Hilary, had a one-to-one session with me. She didn't have a website but I suggested that she should set up a blog, write an article on there that related to her work and her passion, and then tweet about it, linking to the blog URL. She cracked on, set up a free blog, wrote an excellent article, social networked it and, within a couple of days, she had several new clients. If you have a message to share, this is powerful stuff!

FEATURE ARTICLES

So it ought to be easy to write blogs, but what about actual articles written for publishing on a website? These tend to be longer than blogs and can sit on your own website, but can also be placed on many other sites across the internet. There are many 'article sites' where they merely run articles on a huge range of topics such as EzineArticles and Evan Carmichael, to name a few.

Then there are 'How to' sites so if you can give away simple 'How to' ideas, this can be excellent. You can, of course, also pitch articles to editors at newspapers and magazines, but we will look at that a little later. For now, let's assume you are creating an article to publish on one or more websites or blogs, in order to inform, educate, connect with, and attract existing and potential clients.

What subject matter can you choose? What could you write your article about?

The important thing to remember is, this is you speaking to the mainstream. There will be no jargon, no 'in talk' – just a mainstream approach. If you can't think what to write about, just do some brainstorming. In the centre of a piece of paper, or in the form of a mind map, write down the main focus of what you do, perhaps the main benefit you can offer people. Let's say you are a raw food coach and your ideal client is a stressed out overweight woman. One benefit you can bring is increased energy and well-being, so write that phrase in the centre of a page and then think of at least five different angles on that topic, which can be, for example, energy, weight loss, juicing, superfoods. Each of these could then generate another five subtopics, so let's take the angle of energy. You could write an article such as '10 ways to have increased energy', 'The top 5 foods to bring you increased energy', 'Use less energy – don't cook!', 'Eat raw, increase your energy'... lots of ideas.

Now think of another benefit or another angle linked to what you do, so perhaps weight loss, then there's superfoods or juicing for health; each focus of what you know can yield at least seven different articles. It's all about a great title and how you pitch the angle of the piece.

Don't make the mistake of thinking that every article you write must spill all the beans. You may be a nutritionist but you don't have to write about every aspect of nutrition in one article – that would be the book!

Just take one little section or idea (and, wherever possible, ensure that's current, seasonal or relevant to a large group of people). Perhaps you fear that you will be stating the obvious. You may be thinking, "Well doesn't everyone already know this stuff?"

The answer may be no. *You* do! And people fall into the trap of thinking that because they know it, everyone does, but even if raw food is already on your radar, it's nice to be reminded of another angle. Perhaps the reader is already aware of the benefits of healthy eating but just hadn't got round to juicing. If she comes across your article on juicing for health, she just may be inspired to dig out her juicer from her cupboard and create one of the recipes you suggest, then she might click onto your website, accept your free gift or taster (which could be more simple recipes to get started) and from there, she may decide to buy products from you or attend one of your workshops or come to you for coaching... you get the idea, it's just about getting yourself out there. REMEMBER – it's perfectly OK for people to hear the same message in different ways. At the Hay House 'I can do it' conference, I was one of the speakers but I also listened to all of the other speakers. I heard countless motivational talks which reaffirmed the same positive messages over and over, but they were each unique, because each speaker had their own USP, a different take on it.

WHAT COULD YOU EXPECT TO GET FROM WRITING BLOGS OR ARTICLES ?

It's important to stress that you must be realistic. Just because someone signs up to your list doesn't mean they will buy from you. It could be a tiny percentage, but it's a numbers game, and it's important for you to have lots of eyes that will see your business name and you as the expert. In fact, factoid coming up here...

Factoid – it's well documented that people need to see the same message or brand at least seven times before it registers, so in other words, if your ideal client reads your blog, then perhaps sees a little quote from you in a newspaper article, then connects with you on Twitter, by the time you've been on their radar around seven times, you're in! You may strike lucky the very first time around and gain clients and notoriety after one blog, but the point that's worth making is that the more exposure you have in different ways for you and your brand, the more likely it is that you will achieve clients and interested parties, including journalists and producers.

Remember, you may be connecting with that seven per cent who are open to what you're offering, or perhaps the 30 per cent who are aware that they may need you at some point.

It's all time well spent; you can become something of a green writer and recycle your own work!

Here's the really great thing about creating these feature articles – once you have a format that works, it's really easy peasy and, in fact, you don't even have to start from scratch each time.

Let's say, for argument's sake, you write a great article called 'How to lose weight – feel great *and* save money' that sounds quite relatable. By the way, that title tripped off the top of my head using the 'Power of Threes'...

Important tip - for titles or introductory phrases, you can use the Power of Threes...

...three phrases that hang together. Politicians use them all the time, even Tony Blair's famous one – EDUCATION, EDUCATION, EDUCATION - when he couldn't think of three different words, he used the same word three times!

So here's a few key pointers as to how to construct your article. Once you've got your great title, plan what your main points will be:

- You will need at least two good, strong points, but no more than seven. That's because of our 'cognitive' capacity – the amount of capacity in our brain. The magical number is seven, which is why you can remember telephone numbers with seven digits – that's the amount of information we can comfortably handle in one go.

- Write your main arguments as bullet points, then construct an introduction that includes your keywords and phrases relating to the article. Just try and bear in mind the phrases or words that people are googling.

- Expand that information into a good middle section making sure that you have included all those bullet points that you had prepared (no more than seven).

- Then add a closing paragraph, which offers a conclusion and either answers the questions that the reader may have, or perhaps poses another one to get people thinking.

- You will also need to include here any references you have used in the article, including any permissions, quotations etc., which you have used as part of your piece.

- Finally, you'll have a closing section where you can tell the reader about you and what you offer. This might be where you can point them to sign up to receive your free gift/free taster or go to your website.

Read through it all and correct your grammar. It's easy to make grammatical errors, especially when you're writing from the heart and just going with the flow, but it's fine to go back and correct all the mistakes later. If you are going to be placing your article on *ezinearticles.com* or a similar site, then there will be a limit to how many links you can add, which they call 'self serving' so check the rules carefully, but as you aren't being paid for your article, you definitely can include your own biog and website.

Here's the really great bit. You can rewrite your own article, using the same kind of angle, but with a different opening and closing paragraph, and rework the central text so that it reads a little differently. You can get really good at recycling your own work, just by changing some phrases. By changing the title and the opening paragraphs and a little bit of reworking on the main points, you have another article to place on a different article site. The reason for this, of course, is that Google spiders can tell if it's exactly the same article, but if it's different enough, it could get noticed and help push up your rankings in terms of search engine optimisation. Make sure you always include your keywords, the words that relate to your business, which are the words and phrases that people would google if they needed what you offer.

Believe it or not, you can even buy a piece of software to do this for you. Have a look at Instant Article Wizard. For around £60 a year, it's one amazing bit of software. Their marketing blurb says it can gather and dissect research on topics you choose in seconds.

Apparently it can, 'Break the research down into subtopics so you can break your content into relevant sections with ease... Generate paragraphs of content based on the topics... Rewrite the research using the integrated The Best Spinner thesaurus.'

In other words, it actually changes the words you have written for you! I'm not personally recommending it, because I haven't tried it, but it's worth a look if you really want to get masses of articles out there and want to create different content fast.

Should you add images to your articles? I they are on your own website, yes, but for publishing elsewhere online, always check because some article sites want images and some don't. Remember to add some tags to the images. Don't forget that your article, including your images, can and should sit on your own website and/or blog, and if you are linked up with organisations or people running websites where they offer information to consumers interested in your business, then offer them your article for free in return for a credit. Always credit yourself as the writer unless it's someone else from your company who has written it, but in any case, mention your website or blog URL.

E-ZINES

The other very important copy that you ought to be creating regularly is your own newsletter or e-zine. I'd urge you to think of producing one if you don't already, as it's a brilliant way to connect with your audience, your clients and potential clients to let them know what's going on and remind them regularly that you are there.

You can use your e-zine to offer free tasters, gifts or offers, let people know what you have coming up and, of course, you can link them back to your articles and blogs too.

Above all, remember that sharing great content is key. I'm guessing that if you are an expert or passionate about your product or service, and you know you have a message to share, that is meaningful, that can make an impact (hope so!), you already have a wealth of content and information at your disposal. It's simply a case of getting it from inside your head out into the arena so that you can share it with potential clients and buyers. Be inspired to 'Birth the Book', the e-zine, the articles... you always wanted to write. If you really can't write, then speak into a voice recognition program, record audio podcasts or film YouTube videos. You could hire someone to write articles for you, but it's imperative that your 'voice' shines through. Remember, too, that most content can be repurposed. Record a video and then use the audio to create a podcast, use the transcript to create ablog or article which can be chunked down into separate topics for Facebook posts and 140 character snippets for Twitter.

Choose some images to represent your topics and put them up on Instagram, perhaps add a quotation and post it as an inspirational meme on Facebook. When you used several chunks or ideas from one topic, file the topic away; a few months later, you can use it again in a different guise, perhaps taking up the theme and using different images or quotes, or even an update on your progress since you first spoke about that topic. There's nothing unethical about 'recycling' your own content; it's an efficient way of ensuring that new readers and viewers get to access your great tips, advice and ideas.

OTHER CONTENT AND SOCIAL MEDIA

In addition to written content, remember that you can record audio podcasts and videos. Videos account for 69 per cent of consumer traffic and are great for attracting viewers (more about looking great on camera later).

If your business is very visual, Pinterest and Instagram will be critical for attracting potentially interested clients. Some businesses, such as image led fashion brands, use only Instagram and video content to promote their work.

It goes without saying you should use social networking to attract readers, viewers and listeners to your content, in addition to bitesize nuggets of wisdom that you share on Twitter, and the odd video that you share directly to Facebook (always do upload videos direct rather than via YouTube). You can also put the first part of an article or blog post on Facebook and encourage people to come and read more on your website. LinkedIn is the place for indepth articles. Live streaming is becoming more popular too, so you could offer live training sessions and webinars too.

Believe in yourself!

Have faith in your abilities!

Without a humble

but reasonable confidence

in your own powers

you cannot be

successful or happy.

Norman Vincent Peale

STEP 2 - STANDING IN YOUR SPOTLIGHT

Have you ever been asked to speak at an event or meeting and shied away from it, even though you KNOW you have at your fingertips all the information that everyone would just love to hear? Are you unhappy with your presentation at your own classes and workshops? Are you desperate to take your message into schools, the workplace or holistic events, but worried about your body language or the public's perception of you? It's so worth learning the skills you need to allow you to conquer your nerves. It's time to rid yourself of limiting beliefs, find your confidence, and discover how you can be a magnet to an audience, customers and potential clients, without anything holding you back.

Feeling confident to stand in the spotlight certainly doesn't come naturally to everyone. Even if you are the life and soul of the party and always the first leading the karaoke, it may be very different when it comes to giving a speech or a presentation about your work or your personal experience. Believe it or not, surveys show that many people claim they'd rather die than speak in public!

The secrets to confidence building lie in being prepared and learning a few tricks. It is possible to appear confident, even when you're nervous! It may sound widely cosmic and alternative to you, but NLP (Neurolinguistic Programming), TFT (Thought Field Therapy) and EFT (Emotional Freedom Technique) all offer useful tools to assist you in overcoming your fears and feeling really strong and secure with your own message.

We've all been and heard talks and presentations by people who are clearly nervous. They look down the whole time and rely on a PowerPoint presentation. It's staggeringly boring and quite uncomfortable because you can sense their nerves. Good body language is important; what you want to be able to do is beam authority on 'your stage' and become a sought-after speaker, and it will all come down to your stage presence, the energy you give off. Ultimately, it won't matter if you stumble a little or pause for a glass of water; it's all about enthusiasm and passion. No one is interested in merely staring at a PowerPoint presentation, what they want is to be engaged with your authenticity.

It's important for you to learn:

- The secrets to confidence building
- The tricks of appearing confident, even when you're nervous!
- How to beam authority on 'your stage'
- How to construct a talk that's entertaining and informative, and become a sought-after speaker
- The secrets of good body language

Confidence is, of course, a big deal for many people. The idea of public speaking, being interviewed or appearing on screen may terrify you. It's important to know how to build confidence and how to appear confident, even when maybe you aren't.

In fact, even if you don't end up doing a talk or presentation, these skills are brilliant for everyday life too. Being confident for an interview, whether that be for a job or to get your child into a school, or indeed to meet a buyer who may be interested in your products, are transferable skills that will stand you in good stead.

We're also going to look at speaking or giving a presentation, and how to construct a great talk. So let's get straight on with what makes a great speaker or interviewee. It comes down to three things, 'The Three P's'.

PASSION, PREPARATION AND PRESENCE.

In fact, it could be Five P's because the full sentence is – 'With Passion, Preparation and good Presence, you can Proffer an excellent Presentation'.

PASSION

We have already covered this in the overview chapter. I'm assuming you were attracted to this book because you have a message you want to share with the world. In fact, we've identified that it's your DUTY to get it out there. If you are authentic and you know you can help other people with your unique knowledge, skills and products, then I'm guessing that you are passionate and enthusiastic about your 'thing', and it's that passion and enthusiasm that needs to be communicated.

We've all been in conferences or events where a speaker has come onstage, spent ages loading their PowerPoint presentation and then proceeded to keep their head down as they mumble their way through a scripted speech that offers facts and statistics, but absolutely zero passion; it's a complete turn-off! Compare that to someone like Jamie Oliver, who walked onstage at a TED talk, tipped a huge wheelbarrow full of sugar onto the stage and said, "This is the amount of sugar the average child will consume this year!" It's a powerful, memorable statement that will be remembered.

People will connect with you and love to hear what you have to say if you seem enthusiastic. This is obvious, I know, but SO many speakers get it wrong. They think it's enough just to give the info and the facts, but in truth it's your passion for your subject that's of interest. Enthusiasm is contagious, and it all comes back to that same principle – people do business with those they like, know and trust, and if you seem authentic and passionate about your brand, chances are you will carry others along with you. It's how the words are delivered that has the impact on the audience. Let's face it, if you don't sound enthusiastic about the classes you run, the workshops on offer or the products you sell, then you can't expect anyone else to get excited!

Of course, often it will be that you are enthusiastic, but the lack of confidence is so crippling that it stops you from engaging and really showing your passion.

PREPARATION

Preparing your content for an interview, talk or presentation is absolutely crucial, not merely so that you will deliver good solid information, but also because the better prepared you are, the more confident you will appear. Again, it sounds obvious but people miss this bit out. They can sometimes be so concerned they will *sound scripted* that they simply rely on their memory and hope it will all work out. On the other side of the coin is that people have prepared a script but are so attached to simply reading from the script they have put no effort into preparing the delivery of the talk. I'm sure you're aware, if something really sounds like it's being 'read', then it's a turn-off. The audience don't mind if you glance at notes or bullet points, or even read part of your talk, but in order to connect you won't be able to be looking down at a script; eye contact is crucial.

PRESENCE

Presence, often known as 'Stage Presence', is how you present yourself – how you give a presentation, or how you sound when you are being interviewed. Again, we've all been at events or conferences when we feel almost uncomfortable for the person who has taken the stage. We feel a sense of sorrow for them because they seem so terrified and their whole body language seems to be crying out, "I wish I were invisible!"

How we look, our presence (how we present ourselves), is incredibly important, and I don't mean by that we need to be a supermodel or have a super fit body (well, unless that's your USP, of course!), but we just have to look like the 'real deal', we have to look congruent with our own message, like a confident person that the audience can connect with, that they could like, know and trust. We need to beam authenticity.

There are some interesting statistics around Perception (another P to add to our list!), how we perceive others when we see or hear them for the first time. It's thought that over 50 per cent of communication is non-verbal, so for example, when you first come out on stage or onto a TV screen, first impressions count.

Just imagine for a moment you are watching TV and you hear that there's going to be an item about GP surgeries and medical doctors are going to start offering free complimentary treatments (I have a wild imagination, I know!). Your ears prick up and you move towards the TV in order to listen to the interview or discussion. The camera pans over to a doctors' surgery and then focuses on a general practitioner;

he is wearing a white coat and has a stethoscope around his neck, but he is also wearing a big, red nose. In those first few seconds or even perhaps a minute when your subconscious mind was presented with an incongruous message that it wasn't expecting, you were so focused on that red nose and your inner voice was probably saying, *"Why on earth is he wearing a bright red nose? Doesn't he realise that makes him lose all credibility? I definitely wouldn't want him to offer an opinion if I'm ill. I thought this was going to be a serious discussion. Maybe it's a fun charity thing he's involved in, but he would have been better off ditching the comedy angle."* By the time your subconscious inner voice has stopped talking, you have missed several seconds or minutes of what he is saying and may actually hear only a short sound bite. You can't help this kind of reaction, it's entirely subconscious and normal.

It's likely that a few minutes later, you find out that he is doing something charitable for Comic Relief: Red Nose Day, but by then it was too late, you'd missed some of the content. So the key for the person being interviewed or making a presentation is to be really sure that their appearance matches their message, or if indeed they are choosing deliberately to wear some kind of costume for comedy effect, then that must be referenced or pointed out straight away in order to make the viewer comfortable with what they will see – to 'pre-empt' it almost.

When there are no visuals, if you are speaking on the radio, or a podcast or teleseminar, incredibly it's thought in the first few moments of adjustment that 80 per cent of our consciousness and awareness is on the SOUND of the voice, adjusting to whether we can hear and understand, if we have any preconceived ideas about the accent the person is speaking in or the tone. Only when we have processed that and our subconscious mind has accepted it as being congruent with what we are expecting to hear, do we actually start to take in the remaining 20 per cent – to concentrate on the actual content being said.

What are the barriers to gaining confidence in order to be able to share our passion, be fully prepared and have the right presence?

Most of us are born 'confident'. Very young children usually have an exuberance, passion and enthusiasm, and are happy to 'perform' – until self-consciousness kicks in.

The chances are that at some point when you were a child, your confidence took a knock. Perhaps you had to stand up and speak in class and someone laughed, or you tried to tell a joke and no one laughed. Most of us are aware of feelings of being judged, concerned about what people will think of us; this is all back to the power of the subconscious mind. The highly acclaimed author and speaker Cheryl Richardson encourages us to notice our inner critic. She reminds us that if we were to speak to a five-year-old child the way we talk to ourselves, we would be up for abuse! For many people, when they are asked to speak or to be interviewed, the line of talk will go something along the lines of... *"I couldn't do that, I'm a terrible public speaker. I wouldn't look good, everyone would judge my awful clothes and I'm several pounds overweight. I'd never be able to remember anything without reading from a full script and my voice would probably sound really weak and not confident. I can't be interviewed because I just wouldn't get the answers out that I really want to. I'd get all confused and then everyone listening would think I'm stupid"*... and so it goes on.

We've all been there! We all know intimately the inner critic from our subconscious mind. But perhaps, even by investing in this book, you have taken a big step forward. You've acknowledged that you DO have an important message to share, a desire to promote what you do and who you are to a wider audience. If you can now hone it down and drill down to the USP, to the facets of your unique 'diamond', and identify your own unique qualities, then you can start talking to your subconscious mind and to others about your passion, about how you do feel confident to stand on stage or be interviewed about your subject because it's such a thrill for you to talk about something you love and as we have already identified. It's, in fact, your DUTY to get it out there.

When your nerves come into play, the trick is to talk to yourself a different way. Ask yourself whether the fear is really an old fear, linked to a childhood memory, or is it that you fear the criticism of the particular group of people you are going to be speaking to? Whatever it is, challenge yourself, and come up with a new dialogue instead of letting your subconscious destroy your confidence.

When you feel really solid on your preparation, then it becomes unshakable, so it really won't matter if an audience didn't particularly like you or the interviewer seems to ask purposely awkward questions. You will feel that *confidence* in yourself and you know that your message is important, and if the audience seem uninterested, well that's about them, not you.

I remember I was once booked to speak at a conference for the Rotary Club. When I arrived, I realised I was sandwiched between several important celebrities and after dinner speakers, and suddenly

I realised that they had probably booked me because they knew I was a co-presenter on *Steve Wright in the Afternoon* on Radio 2 and they knew I interviewed lots of big stars and celebs. I started to panic; I was there to talk about holistic living and offer tips and ideas from my first book, *Imperfectly Natural Woman*, and so hadn't prepared anything else. My subconscious mind literally 'went off' telling me that I'd be mocked. *"There's no way this audience want to hear about eco laundry products and organic skincare,"* I thought. *"The speaker before me is award-winning actress Dame Anna Neagle!"* my inner voice reasoned.

I told myself they would feel I was totally incongruent and out of touch with them; the audience was mostly middle-aged men and a few of their wives.

Suddenly, I stopped my subconscious chatter in its tracks and said to myself, or possibly out loud, *"I'm passionate about my message, I know I will deliver an informative and entertaining talk, and if it's not what they were expecting, well hey, surprise!"* I practised a few NLP techniques, calmed down and visualised myself as a success.

Well guess what? I went out there, hit them with half an hour of tips and ideas for everything from avoiding the artificial sweetener aspartame to the importance of ditching the chemicals, using bicarbonate of soda and white vinegar for cleaning, and how you can make a great facial scrub with oatmeal, and though I say so myself, I rocked it!

Embarrassingly, the next speaker had to be delayed because there was such a massive queue to buy my book. I sold all 300 copies I'd taken along with me, and could probably have sold more!

If I had let my nervous subconscious chatter destroy my confidence, I dread to think what would have happened. I did, however, quickly 'reassess' my talk. I delivered the same talk but with a 'nod' towards the audience; this is sometimes called doing a quick audience analysis. In this case, all I did was up my 'entertainment' value, threw in a gag or two about working with celebrities, and left out the section on the importance of breastfeeding! Effective speakers and communicators do 'read' their audience and match their behaviour. As you walk into the room, you can decide whether to warm them up a bit and connect with them, telling a bit of an impromptu story as you set up your laptop or whatever, or if they are shuffling in their seats wanting to really get on with it, you can do just that.

Destructive inner talk can so easily affect us. Really look at what your fears are. Perhaps you're saying to yourself, *"I'll stumble on some of my phrases,"* or, *"I'll be clumsy and drop my glass of water or my papers"*. Try and remember that from the audiences perspective, they won't notice the stumbling. They will only connect with the passion that you have for your subject, how real you are, whether you seem likeable, and like someone they could get to know and trust, and so what if you spill the water, you're human!

Most of you are well aware of the subconscious mind and the various tools and techniques that we can use to literally reprogramme the way we think, and if you are new to all of this, think about getting some more help and training.

HOW TO BEAM CONFIDENCE

THE TRICKS TO APPEARING POSITIVE AND HAVING GOOD BODY LANGUAGE

How you stand is important. When I work one-to-one with people, I often ask them to stand in an imaginary spotlight, really be grounded and feel their feet firmly on the floor, no crossing legs or swaying. You need a strong position, head up, breathing calmly.

Don't look down at your script or notes constantly, but also do not look over the heads of the audience. Most of the time, try and make eye contact, actual eye contact with first one person, then another, around the room.

It's fine to look at notes, take a sip of water, look down occasionally as you pause for breath, but for the majority of the time, make eye contact.

If you are familiar with NLP, there are some wonderful exercises to help boost confidence directly before an interview or presentation. Anyone familiar with NLP knows how great it is to have an 'anchor' to really help get you into the right state before you need to present.

PREPARATION

The amount you prepare has a direct effect on how your presentation will go. There are two elements to preparation, the actual content/construction of the talk. and practising the delivery. Let's talk about the content first.

It's all back to remembering what's unique about you. We talked earlier about the fact that it's your DUTY to share your message with a wider community if you have that desire and we really want to get in touch with what are the core messages. What's special about you? What's your USP? Once you are clear on that, it becomes easier to construct a talk and ensure that you are prepared and confident to present to and engage with the media and your potential future clients. People buy on emotion and justify with fact.

I heard this described as 'searching for your Diamond'. It's a lovely analogy but it really sums up what we need to seek out, that Gem that is within us. You may feel like a whole mine of unrelated gemstones and be totally unclear what your message is, how to show your passion and how to feel confident, but this is a great way of digging it out.

In one of the exercises later in this book, I'm going to ask you to sing your own praises, to write down all the great things about you, your achievements, successes, skills, talents, anything quirky.

I ask you to draw a heart in the centre of a piece of paper and write your name within the heart, because I'm assuming you have a 'heart-centred' business. What's interesting is that some of the media star clients working with me personally found that in retrospect they hadn't actually written down anything that was 'personal'. In several instances, they wrote down what they can do for others but didn't really 'show off'. If you remember I suggested you add to that list, not just your business credentials such as *"I'm great at inspiring others,"* or *"I can transform teenagers,"* etc., but also to add in the fun stuff, *"I can make an awesome apple pie,"* and *"I'm proud that I crocheted a scarf that my mum is wearing...I can always find great scarves in charity shops,"* It's important because it's all YOU, and all these little qualities are important in making up the whole.

I'd like you to take that exercise one step further and imagine that the heart in the centre of the page has morphed into a gemstone, any kind of precious stone. Draw some lines coming out from it to show that it's sparkling and then write down some words associated with that, the gem that is within you. The word 'diamond', of course, links to 'precious, unique, rare, a thing of beauty,' and the really important bit – it has many facets. From that, you can start to equate your 'gem' your pearl of wisdom. You can ask, "What is 'unique' about me? What is this one true gem that I can share?" When you really get in touch with your Unique Brilliance (YOU-nique Brilliance), and you know that you are a mine of information with a few real clear gems that you can share your unique take on, then you will start to feel more confident about putting yourself out there as a speaker or an interviewee, and the clearer you are about what you want to convey to your audience.

Imagine you have been asked to give a presentation, a 20 minute talk. Decide who the audience is and the theme. For a talk of just 20 minutes, it's going to be about one clear idea. You'll be able to impart one real GEM from within you, and a few other facets, but what is that gem that you want to share?

So in order to create the content, or the script for your presentation or talk, first choose your 'gem', your angle. Now you need to know how to piece it together so that it flows.

Let's look at constructing a talk or presentation. It must have a solid construction or format otherwise it will be simply disjointed ideas that don't hang together.

Try and think of your talk as a journey. There is a 'system' that many speakers use, a kind of flow that works well and keeps the interest for the listener. It will usually be an opening introductory section, which works well if it's something personal or a story to set the scene, then the key themes develop as you start to reveal the various factors until you reach the peak, the 'climax' if you like. This is the point at which you really hammer your message home; you may have been building up to it from the outset, or it may be that here is where you really deliver the defining moment. From there is a descent to the end, via a conclusion, perhaps a summary and an end, which is often a call to action, with clear guidelines as to how to get in contact or do something different.

The journey from the outset to the conclusion takes the listener from A to B. The old adage is, *'Tell them what you are going to tell them, tell them it, and then tell them what you have told them'*.

Get real clarity on your Purpose and the one key message you want to share. You'll need to brainstorm the topics around your main purpose and think what the audience might want to hear from you.

So let's look at that structure again...

Good talks usually start with a defining story, so rather than just offer a factual introduction to the talk you are going to give, it's good to include something personal at the outset. Something memorable such as you 'Telling them what you are going to tell them' and then your bullet point ideas (remember, never more than seven) can be dotted through as you hold the attention of the audience, building to a kind of climax of your talk. You are building to your ONE Main point... your 'gem'.

As you move into your theme, you may want to build in some kind of suspense and drama to keep the energy, and the climax could be the one 'killer fact' that we've been waiting for or the joke or punchline – whatever it is for you. Then you can really drill home your message and have what's sometimes called a 'Call to Action' where you are engaging the audience in some way or inviting them to be willing to make a change or think differently after the talk you've just delivered. The conclusion will be the reminder of what you've said – telling them what you told them. Ideally then, 10 per cent of the time will be for the intro, the warm-up story, 80 per cent the main meat of the talk, and the last 10 per cent for the conclusion and call to action, if there is one.

Most people make their talks too full of information. People often fall into the trap when giving a talk or presentation of thinking that they need to tell the audience everything they know. They feel they must deliver all the facts in order to give great value, but the interesting thing is we can only retain so much, and people remember the information if it's in the form of a story. You know how I told you about my experience at the Rotary Club event? Well that was a story to illustrate how even if you feel the audience aren't right for you, you can stand in your power and do what you were going to do anyway. Use the power of emotion; if you try and remember the name of your neighbour's pet from many years ago, your brain will probably struggle to recall it, but try and remember your first kiss, and unless you've consciously blocked it out because it was so terrible, you'll probably find an easier recall! So from the audience perspective, any stories or emotions you convey are more likely to be remembered than facts and figures. The audience will connect and hopefully will come to like, know and trust you.

Another interesting technique speakers sometimes use is a structure based around a question or a problem, or indeed both sides of an argument can be presented.

Remember, if you are authentic, there are many ways to present your message, but above all, it must be powerful, not 'wishy washy'. The best talks or presentations leave the audience very clear about the key messages and clear about what they could do differently, or could feel inspired to do.

LESS IS MORE

Don't make the mistake of thinking you have to give masses of content from the stage. In the past, I've definitely been guilty of that. I've given an hour long talk on reducing synthetic chemicals in household products and personal care products, and I was convinced that I needed to pack in as many recommendations as possible to give great value. Ironically, people would leave my talks completely overwhelmed, some would buy my books, many would email me and ask specific questions, but in some cases, I think I had merely stirred something up, and ultimately left people out on a limb, unsure where to start and possibly after being 'talked at' for an hour, they may have even felt, *"It's all too much, what's the point?"*

It really isn't necessarily to speak for too long. Truthfully, the shortest talks are the most difficult to prepare for, as at first you can't imagine what you will be able to leave out, but Winston Churchilll said, *"A good speech should be like a woman's skirt; long enough to cover the subject and short enough to create interest"* (ahem!)

I learnt my lesson and when I gave a talk at the Hay House 'I can do it' conference, I did it differently. I won't reveal all in case I offer a similar talk and you are in the audience, but it's save to say several people have told me that, despite the length of my skirt but because of the 1950's apron and headscarf I donned and the toilet brush I wielded, they remembered the talk and made it their business to do further research and read my books.

It's important to remember that an audience can only retain so much, especially facts and figures. Our cognitive brain can only handle around seven pieces of information at a time, but if you verbally paint a picture or tell a story, that uses a different part of the brain and it's more easily retained. It's not the facts and statistics that are important, they can be checked later, it's the stories that they can identify with, the anecdotes that made them laugh, the comments you made that made them relate to you, the questions that challenged their long held beliefs. A reminder again – the format needs to go along the lines of ...'Tell them what you are going to tell them (intro), tell them (the main body of the story building to a 'climax'), tell them what you told them (recap), and finish with a conclusion and, if relevant, a call to action.' Be very clear as to what you want people to do or feel as a result of your talk; you may end with a challenge, a question or a definite call to action – inviting people to sign up to buy your product or service, but whatever you do, don't let the talk just fizzle out. Ensure it's a punchy ending and the audience are clear that you have finished – hopefully that will trigger the applause!

When you have got your idea, your themes and your structure, you'll need a good title.

Now this can notoriously difficult! My best suggestion is that you have a look at some of the TED talks; always intriguing and awesome titles. (Just google TED talks and you'll find them.)

So when you have all the ideas, how do you script it? You do exactly that, initially. I know, it sounds arduous, but I do script it all out, literally write down every word. The trick here is to write how you speak. You may think, *"That's crazy! I can't read the script out in front of an audience so why write it all?"* Well it's all in the preparation. If you write it out, you are helping your visual memory. If that really doesn't work for you, or it's a long presentation, then just write out the sections, clearly with bullet points. Of course, you won't be able to read from a script when you are on stage, but you can glance down at bullet point cards. The script is purely for your rehearsal. Once you've read through the script word for word a couple of times, you are ready to then chunk it down to sections and eventually to bullet points on cards.

Make sure you write your script 'for speech' i.e. write the words in the way that they would be spoken. I can't emphasise this enough. Write any tricky long words phonetically and mark up on your own script any words that you often stumble on. Just by marking it with a pen, it gives a sort of heads up to your subconscious mind to give a tiny bit of extra attention when you come to that word.

Which brings us to ….

PREPARATION FOR DELIVERY OF THE TALK

I'm always amazed how many people think it's OK to give a speech having never read it through out loud. Similarly, people show up for radio interviews having never rehearsed their main points out loud. Reading through your speech or script out loud is crucial. Why? Because you need to get your muscles working. Can you imagine heading out to run a marathon without training? Of course not! You need to use the same muscles in the same way and for the same length of time, ideally in similar conditions over the same route. Your voice is no different. When you practice saying certain words in a certain order, the mouth knows how to get around the shapes!

Saying words out loud also helps with memory retention. If you really can't speak out loud, then move your lips silently. In a study published in the *Journal of Consciousness and Cognition*, Professor Victor Boucher from the University of Motreal said, "The simple fact of articulating without making a sound creates a sensorimotor link that increases our ability to remember, but if it is related to the functionality of speech, we remember even more."

If you were to be in a theatre green room where auditions were taking place, the actors would be waiting for their turn, and it would not look like a doctor's waiting room with everyone quietly reading or looking at their audition script. The actors would be pacing around, using available corridor space to warm up, to literally warm up their vocal chords, and get their mouth physically moving around the words they were going to be delivering when their turn to perform came. Similarly, backstage before any concert performance, singers warm up their voice and sing some lines from their repertoire; it's 'muscle memory' and it's critical. On my PR and Media Skills Masterclass courses, I remind participants that our voice is an instrument and if we practice, we can use it to great effect.

The key to relieving tension is to breathe. We need plenty of oxygen in our bloodstream so it's really important to breathe well but not overbreathe as that will cause a feeling of panic.

Sometimes it's enough just to remember not to stop breathing, because when we are nervous, we can tend to hold our breath.

VOICE TECHNIQUE
PITCH, PACE, PAUSE AND POWER

Pitch is not something you should worry about, unless you know that you have a tendency to speak in a rather too high pitch. This can happen when we get nervous. The answer is to be aware of it, and breathe; when you combine this with the other confidence building tips, usually once you are aware, you can consciously lower your voice.

Pace, the speed at which you speak. Again, if you know that you have a tendency to speak much too fast when under pressure, breathe, focus, and visualise yourself speaking at the correct pace. It's important to remember that audio is not like print media. If someone is hearing you on the radio or giving a talk, they can't whizz their eyes back and read that bit again the way you can when reading a newspaper article. Once it's said, it's 'out' and so clarity is important. Ensure that you don't speak so fast that the audience can't grasp the words.

Pause. Now again, if you think of a paragraph of writing, punctuation helps to break it up and create emphasis in the right place. We use commas, semicolons and full stops. In speech, the pause is our one fabulous punctuation tool, and we can use it to great effect. It's perfectly OK to pause to effect... to pause to collect your thoughts. Pauses are critically important.

Power is another way of emphasising certain points. We can literally STRESS certain words. In your notes, write what you want to stress in capital letters so that when it comes to that extra important piece of info, you will remember to... pause and give that word more POWER.

So practice your script out loud, noticing whether you speed up or slow down, time yourself, and ensure that you won't go over time.

Think about your posture too. Don't always practice your talk sitting down; walk around or stand as you would on the stage. When I work with people one-to-one, I sometimes get them to stand as if in a spotlight and get in touch with that feeling of standing tall and feeling powerful, beaming out authority. That feeling of strength comes from being in touch with your authenticity, that gem inside you that you are going to deliver to the audience.

'I'VE LEARNED THAT PEOPLE FORGET WHAT YOU SAID, PEOPLE WILL FORGET WHAT YOU DID, BUT PEOPLE WILL NEVER FORGET HOW YOU MADE THEM FEEL' MAYA ANGELOU

You must expect great things of yourself before you can do them.

Michael Jordan

STEP 3 - BE A GREAT INTERVIEWEE, PART 1 - SOUND GREAT!

In my work on radio, so many times I've seen professionals simply 'blow' their golden opportunity to get their message out to sometimes millions of listeners, merely because they don't know the techniques and tricks for being a GREAT interviewee. Often, if it's pre-recorded, we've actually had to 'dump' the interview! It was a situation like this that led me to start doing this work; offering coaching, sharing tips and ideas to help people with a great message to share, to get it across.

It's not enough just to rock up at an interview, whether audio or visual, even if you are offering a short comment on an Internet podcast. It's imperative that you get your preparation right and be clear on your agenda. It's important to be clear on the agenda of the interviewer too. Establish what the angle of the piece is. Who are the target audience? Once you've answered these questions, remember within that framework that YOUR message and YOUR agenda comes across how you want it to. It sounds way too obvious, but when you are first asked to take part in an interview in addition to establishing the date, whether the interview is live or recorded etc., also ask about the agenda and if you are being interviewed alongside another interviewee or are going to be part of a debate. Always find out who that person is and ensure that you know their views. In case you are asked to give an interview at short notice, do the following exercises and make sure you are clear on your key messages that you will want to get across. Know your key messages inside and out so that whatever questions are thrown at you, they can be acknowledged and then gently manoeuvred in order for you to say what you wanted to say anyway. This is an art – listen to politicians!

HOW DO YOU SOUND NATURAL ON RADIO?

You need to authentically feel as though you are 'connected' and having a conversation with the listener. It's all about how people perceive your voice. The listener wants to hear someone they can feel a bond with; someone they can like, know and trust.

<u>Now, an important point here.</u> If you are know you are going to be speaking on radio, *don't try and adopt another voice*; keep your own accent, and don't try and be anything that you aren't. The enthusiasm in your voice is what's needed.

Don't forget that if you are on radio, you think of it as if you are talking to one person. If you train as a radio broadcaster, you are taught earlier on to never say, "All you listeners out there..." You speak as if you are just talking to one.

It is disconcerting because you are often in a studio all alone staring at brick walls, usually not even a window. Then you start to imagine the thousands or millions of people potentially listening, even though it feels as though no one is listening.

When I first started presenting, this freaked me out a bit, but I knew I must focus on the audience – the ONE person – so I decided on my 'ideal listener' at that time. I decided my ideal person was a London cabbie.
I was producing and presenting a show on gospel music and inspirational music but I didn't want the mainstream audience to

switch off; I wanted it to appeal to everyone, so I cut out a photo from a newspaper of a guy driving a London cab and stuck it on the desk in front of me. I spoke directly to him and it really helped me focus. Of course, if you are being interviewed, you need to talk merely to the person or the people who are interviewing you, but please remember not to say, "All you out there..." The interesting thing about radio is that it is like a friend; people love listening to the radio because it's informative, entertaining or comforting, and usually if they get to like a presenter, even though they are aware that there are many other millions of people listening, they still feel that they are the only ones listening – and that's how it should be.

Remember, the same rules apply to any audio you create, be that your own podcasts, audio products, or on the airwaves.

WHAT DOES THE INTERVIEWER WANT FROM YOU ?

I'd like to tell you a bit about how it is from the point of view of the interviewer, which might help you shape your interview. When I was working at a local BBC station, my job was to set up my own show in its entirety. I had no producers, researchers, assistants, or even studio engineers. I had to research guests, ring them up to book them, and ensure that I was able to deliver interesting, relatable interviewees to my target audience. It was a fine line. I needed to invite people who were of interest to my audience, but usually they were willing to come and be interviewed only when they had something to promote.

If you are at a national radio station or a bigger local one as a presenter, you may be lucky enough to have a producer and/or researcher who will sort out the guests for you, and draft some possible questions and a few production notes about the guest, but it's important to remember that the presenter has to do hundreds of interviews and it's unlikely that he or she will have read your book in full, or be fully genned up on what you do. In fact, some might say that if he is too intrinsically entwined with what you do, it won't be a good journalistic interview. The presenter's job is to ask the questions that the public, the listeners, will want to hear. It's not the job of the presenter to already know about your topic in depth or to 'sell' what you do, but it is the job of a good interviewer to ask incisive questions that facilitate you to give important information.

When I started my Hay House radio shows, I was given the details of the authors I had to interview and sent their books, but it felt like an overwhelming amount of work for me to do, to read the books in full, because several of them aren't authors I was familiar with. So I emailed the authors and asked them to send me their ideal introduction; how they would like to be introduced? What seven 'dream questions' would they like to be asked? Obviously from that starting point, that triggered my brain to come up with some great questions that they weren't necessarily expecting, but nevertheless gave them the opportunity to promote their books in an even more interesting way.

Above all, the interviewer wants to know what the listener wants to know. They want relatable information, interesting, fun or even controversial.

They want the low-down from you. You'll have heard of the classic 'journo questions' – Who, What, Where, Why, When, How? Make sure you have an answer for those questions, even though you may not be asked them and not necessarily in that order!

Remember we spoke of choosing your themes? Have absolute clarity on your specific angle for the interview. It's unlikely that if you are a nutritionist, the interview is just about food and nutrition; there will be an angle, and if there isn't, I suggest you choose one and decide upon it, something current, something that everyone is talking about. You need one or two key ideas, key things that you are passionate about getting across, and no more than seven supporting arguments (so as not to conflict with the cognitive capacity of the brain).

Ensure that you have your main key theme and idea (or two max), then seven supporting ideas/themes. Think ahead to what the interviewer might ask you. Go through the Who, What, Where, Why, When, How questions and check that if any are appropriate to your topic that you have the answer; have them well-prepared and up your sleeve.

LET'S LOOK AT PREPARING YOUR CONTENT. YOUR AGENDA.

We've all seen politicians being interviewed. They've usually had copious amounts of media training and are hot at sticking to their agenda, despite any awkward questions. You'll have heard them in full swing; a very persuasive interviewer will say something along the lines of, "You must be absolutely devastated that you lost such a high proportion of seats in your constituency in last night's election," and you will never hear them reply, "We are devastated." It will always be a quick acknowledgment, then, "Here's the really exciting thing. This heralds the start of an exciting new time for us..."

A while back, there was the police commissioner elections in the UK, and the lack of publicity and general apathy led to as few as five per cent of people casting their votes. It was all across the newspapers, seen as catatosrophic disaster, and yet when I heard a radio news clip of, I think it was David Cameron the Prime Minister, his sound bite was, "Low turnout? I think it bodes well for the future. At least three million people have had a say in this important issue!"

I'm not suggesting you plan for confrontational policitic-style interviews. But if the interview does become in any way aggressive or confrontational, avoid saying, "No comment." Always answer the question to the best of your ability. Be truthful; if you don't know the answer to a specific question, admit that. If it's something you know you ought to know, offer to find out and come back, but don't speculate, stumble or procrastinate if you haven't got facts to hand. Some will remember the disastrous interview by the Green Party leader in the run-up to the last General Election campaign. Many press reports considered it was the nail in the coffin for the party' she was 'annihilated,' they said, by a radio broadcaster. It was the most uncomfortable three or four minute of radio I have ever listened to. She claimed afterwards she had suffered 'brain freeze'. Personally, I believe she had simply not done the preparation necessary.

What's important is that you do need your own agenda, but ultimately unless you really are a politican, you will need to find a clever and subtle way of keeping it conversational.

Remember that an interview is not an exam

When you were at school, you were no doubt told you must answer all papers and oral tests exactly as they are asked. Indeed, in an exam paper, it's imperative that you answer the actual question asked. There's that classic line in the old movie and stage play, *Educating Rita* by Willy Russell, where Julie Walters is marked down or fails because when the exam paper asked for an essay (the subject was to suggest a solution to the problems encountered by stage directors of Henrik Ibsen's *Peer Gynt*), her one-line essay was, "Do it on the radio". That tells us something about sound bites too!

The point I'm making is that **interviews are not exams, they are conversations**, so therefore questions must be acknowledged but not necessarily (unless perhaps it is a matter of international significance and you are a politician) have to be answered, or at least not directly.

The best analogy is that of **a tennis game**. If you imagine that the interviewer is in one part of the court and you are in the opposite corner, they serve the ball i.e. they put out a question. The ball goes literally into your court, then you have two options: serve it directly back i.e. a direct answer to the question, or run across to the other side of the court, then send it back; in other words, acknowledge the question then answer in a way that reflects your own agenda. What this does is open up the conversation. A good interviewer will be delighted if you take the conversation in a slightly different direction so long as it's interesting for his or her listeners and it's in some way relevant or deliberately irrelevant to the topic. So if you really want to get a point across, find a way of leading the interviewer in that direction.

The trick is to have your key themes ready. Have your agenda – or you may prefer to call it your topics – two key points and then no more than seven supporting points, and get good at pre-empting what questions you are likely to be asked and how. If you were asked them, you could acknowledge them and perhaps run with the ball, or the question, to another bit of the court before you lob it back.

Listen to the interviewer while they are asking the question. It's important to listen. You may be feeling nervous before he gets to you, but listen to how he introduces you – you may get a clue as to what he's expecting –and listen during the questions or you may find yourself confused!

It's hugely important to make eye contact directly with the interviewer. He or she may be fiddling with equipment, but try to keep eye contact the whole time.

Give yourself time to respond. Don't be rehearsing your own agenda while the questions are being asked. Listen to his questions but be mindful of how you can acknowledge it, and then respond.

If you need a breathing space, start slowly by saying, "It's a good question..." or "It's not a question I was expecting, but..." Usually, the acknowledgment gives your brain the time it needs to kick into gear and remind you of a prepared bullet point, or indeed just a relevant answer to the interviewer's question.

Always be prepared with a good example or story. Remember by telling a story, however short, you engage the listener. Also remember that audio is just that, audio only. There are no visuals, so you can help the listener by painting pictures. What I mean by that is especially if you are passing on stats, numbers or anything tricky is hard to hear in an instant. Remember we spoke about how when we read a newspaper and if there's a statistic that we don't quite catch it, we can go back and reread it? For example, if a newspaper sentence read, "A new monument 8.76 metres high has just been unveiled in a local park". If your brain flagged up that you weren't sure how high that was, you might reread the numbers while you literally try and figure out how high that really is, but in audio terms, the words are out and that's it, so instead you could say, "A new monument the size of two double-decker bus has been unveiled." Ah, now I can imagine the size!

If you are using statistics, it's a great idea to equate with images that are relatable. If you want to quote a statistic, such as "It's estimated that 83,000 people each year apply for complimentary therapies on the NHS", (by the way, these are not real statistics) it might be better to add, "That's enough people interested in complimentary therapies to fill Wembley Stadium," so that the listener can form a picture of that number of people.

You can also be emotive or use metaphors to get your point across, but keep sentences relatively short.

If you are asked a very challenging or provocative question, give yourself time. Use the pause, be calm and don't rise to any bait. Remember, it's not an exam.

DEALING WITH NERVES

Getting your 'plugs' in? You will need to find a way of referring to your business or website without being too overt. Usually a good interviewer will credit you fully at the beginning and end of an interview. If you have a book out, they will most definitely give the details of the book. But what no one wants is to hear is a guest gratuitously getting their plugs in all the way through the interview.

Preparation of your key messages is critical, so that you can 'take control' (without sounding as if you are, of course!). When you know the angle of the interview, it's not usually difficult to pre-empt what some of the questions will be, rehearse your answers in advance, learning your own message off by heart, and knowing how to say it in several different ways. You won't be able to have notes in front of you at an interview. It's hugely important, even on radio, to keep constant eye contact with the interviewer, so the most you could have is a card with three or four bullet points, single words ideally, as a crib sheet in case, like that unfortunate Green Party leader, you get brain freeze.

Don't confuse that with nerves. It's likely you will feel a little nervous, which is a good thing, but when you are fully prepared, even if you did 'freeze', it would be for a nanosecond only, and as soon as you glance down and see one word written in capital letters, that will click your subconscious mind back into gear and you will be back on track, with a pause that no one will have noticed. That's why most theatre companies hire a prompt for their actors; not to prop them up by constantly feeding them lines (the actor will always know the lines thoroughly because of this rigorous preparation), but if they were to 'freeze' and forget momentarily, the prompt would remind them of the next few words and they would be able to continue.

With the content preparation for your interview, don't forget the importance of a good 'sound bite'. If your interview is pre-recorded, it may well be edited down to just one clip, so make sure every sentence counts! If it's live, it of course won't be edited, but you may find yourself with a short time to sum up or you may find a sound bite from the interview is clipped and replayed. Make sure that what you say still stands, even if taken in isolation!

A sound bite is exactly that; a nugget, a key point or punchy phrase that can be pulled out of the whole and can stand alone. It needs to be powerful and succinct. The bottom line is that you need to be interesting and 'quotable'. If you do the following exercise, hopefully you will know what your 'tag line' is, and you will be able to sum up your key message in 10 words or less. Using Twitter is a good exercise too; keeping to 140 characters (preferably less to allow for links) is a great discipline to help you get your message across in as few words as possible. Let's face it, we are living in a society where we have a depleting attention span!

In addition to preparing your content, think about your preparation for an audio interview too. Make sure that you get some advice on breathing and voice techniques to make you confident in the way you sound, and recognise the importance of the breath, especially if you're feeling nervous.

Nothing great was ever achieved without enthusiasm.

Ralph Waldo Emerson

STEP 4 - BE A GREAT INTERVIEWEE, PART 2 - LOOK GREAT!

O nce you've mastered the art of speaking and communicating 'from the heart', it's important to recognise the techniques of **visual presentation**. It's becoming more and more important to present yourself well in order to affect people's perception of you and your brand. Undoubtedly, times have changed and the good news is we can ALL now compete with the likes of the huge multinationals on a level playing field. Whether you're making YouTube productions for your own 'sole trader' business, acting as a spokesperson for your company, or as an interviewee in any situation, be it in front of your web, smartphone camera or a TV camera, you don't have to be beautiful... just 'right' – congruent as a representation of your brand, and it's really worth ensuring that you create a powerful impression in front of a camera.

It doesn't need to break the bank, and you no longer need to hire expensive teams. There are very cost-effective ways to make your own presentation, and it's important to research the best equipment that's easy.

I've already written about Perception. I will just remind you that perception is everything; at least 80 per cent is visual, so in order for the subconscious mind to accept that you look congruent with what was being expected, if you remember I gave the example of the news story about a doctor in a surgery, if he is wearing a red nose (despite the fact that this may get explained later in the piece if he discusses his charity work for Red Nose Say), the problem is that the subconscious mind is so caught up with the inner talk about the incongruent messages, it's likely that the actual content or at least the opening lines will be missed.

When you are in vision, you will be in view at all times so it's essential that you remember that. When we discussed being interviewed on radio, we said it's OK to have some notes with bullet points on the table in front you, but that isn't possible on camera. While you're on, you are literally on. Having said that, when I was a guest on *The Wright Stuff* on Channel 5, we were allowed one card on which we could add a couple of bullet point notes, but generally on televison or on camera, it just doesn't look right to be looking down at cards or paper, unless, of course, reading something from a cue sheet is part of the content.

It's unlikely you will have an autocue, that's usually the main presenters, so if you can't have your notes, what then? Well fortunately, most TV interview are very short and very clear on their angle, so in terms of preparing your content, you will need to have one clear point and be clear on your arguments around it.

If you are the main presenter on a programme or even just a vlog that feels important to keep to script, you could choose autocue. Reading from an autocue is a skill all of its own, as you need to be able to scan text and yet not look as though you are moving your eyes too much. If you are recoding your own promo videos and it's not possible to learn your script, then you can get autocue programmes for your iPad or computer, but you do need to careful of the positioning as unlike the professional ones in TV studios, they won't be intrinsic to the camera so your eyeline and focusing can be out of kilter.

WHAT TO WEAR

Being on camera is just like being on stage. It IS a performance and if you are in vision, it's actually not OK to just rock up in your jeans and scruffy hair and hope that your words of wisdom will make the right impression. You need to present your very best self on camera. There are a few body language secrets, but it ultimately comes down to how well you have prepared.

Clients of mine often agonise about what to wear on TV and video. You want to create the perfect image for your brand, but often it's the simplest things that work best on camera. For the gals, avoid jangly jewellery; it will get in the way of the microphone, which will be clipped to you. If you are the kind of person that usually wears big dangly earrings, be careful, as on camera they can look like scrap metal.

For the guys, make sure your keys aren't jingling in your trouser pocket! Think carefully about the clothes you choose. Jules Standish, style and colour consultant, explains how important the use of colour is. It's usually not a great idea to wear black on TV, especially not close to your face, as it will drain the colour away and often isn't flattering. Jules' book *How not to wear black* really helps to explain the psychology of colour and how certain colours work for us. She talks of how blue is a great colour for communication; so many TV and radio presenters choose blue.

In terms of colours and patterns to avoid, nothing too 'messy' works. Avoid dynamic patterns. Vibrant stripes can start to give a strobing effect on TV, as can brilliant white, so sometimes producers will advise on colours that would be good. Daft as it may seem too, ake sure you tone with the set. When I was working on *The Wright Stuff* on Channel 5, I always tried to make sure my outfits worked alongside the colourful sofa we sat on!

On TV, avoid wearing anything that's too low cut - if you are exposing flesh, remember you will need to carry your make-up base down onto the neck and chest area too. Similarly, if you are wearing short sleeves, then the colour of your arms matches your face if you are wearing make-up that gives you a darker tone.

Wearing make-up on camera is important, in order to even out skin tone, and tone down any redness or high colour because that's exaggerated on camera. It's not about looking 'made-up' or changing how you want to appear, just about enhancing the real you. In fact, good make-up doesn't look like you are made up at all! If have dark areas or circles around eyes, they could be accentuated on camera and look shadowy without make-up, so it's good to use a good coverage make-up in small quantities.

Men often ask if they must wear make-up too. Yes, if you're in a brightly lit studio and especially if you are seated next to a female guest or presenter, otherwise you would look very bland compared to them. If you know you tend to have a high colour when nervous, then a light foundation or powder will sort it. Remember, good make-up shouldn't be seen.

Most people need light powder on the T-zone area of the face because if you look too shiny under the lights, that's disconcerting.

It's important to look well-groomed, not too messy. Even if you usually have the hippy chick scruffy look, make sure your eyebrows are groomed, that you look clean and fresh; zits don't work on TV! Any uneven skin tones will be distracting; remember, it's all about perception. If this irks you because you're thinking, "Hold on, I'm not a model or beauty queen, I'm a serious authentic entrepreneur," well that's the point. In order to grasp your authenticity, we need to hear your content and see your smile. Our subconscious minds need the image to be well-presented, to be congruent, and I will stress again, that doesn't mean ladening on bright pink lipstick when you never normally wear a scrap of make-up. It's just about making your sking tone look even, and looking well-presented.

Hair must be tidy on camera as we need to be able to see your eyes. Hair needs to be 'dressed' in the true sense of the world, so not drowning your face. At one time, most TV studios had hair and make-up artists; now you will usually still be offered it on breakfast TV shows but many smaller shows, and of course, outside broadcasts, etc. won't have make-up facilities so it's worth taking a small kit with you, a small mirror and some essentials.

Make-up can also help to boost confidence. A colleague, who had opportunity to be filmed by QVC, didn't feel confident. She was expecting a make-up person, and just hadn't considered there wouldn't be one. Her hair was in her face while she was recording, and when she saw the video back, her hair was in her eyes andshe wished she had given it more thought.

On camera, you need to exude confidence so wear something you feel good in and make sure make-up is neat and looks good.

WHY YOU MUST GET ON CAMERA, AND THE TECHY BIT...

I've already stressed the importance of being seen on camera – it's the number one way to engage with your tribe. Remember...

Approximately four billion videos are viewed daily online

75 per cent of those are viewed from a smartphone

90 per cent of those are under three minutes long

The techy side of video is not my area, but I do know it doesn't need to break the bank; you can shoot from your iPhone (get a plug-in microphone) or invest in a decent camera. The audio is important, so record 30 seconds and then check it back. Check the environment; white walls can be too stark so op for some texture in the background, a plant or soft furnishings (which will help with the sound too), but the lighting is key; aim for natural daylight wherever possible, or add in some light. You can buy lights cheaply – get a tutorial on how to use it to avoid shadows.

Stick to the rule of three for the framing, i.e. imagine the screen is split horizontally into thirds, and ensure that your eyeline is framed in the top third of the screen. Always shoot in landscape format.

PHOTOGRAPHIC IMAGES

Of course, it goes without saying that you need a good headshot photograph too, preferably one professionally taken in a studio which shows you as you really are. By that, I don't mean you can't look your best, but I'm not talking about a highly glamourised pic that has been massively photoshopped. The purpose of the headshot is so that people can check that you look authentic and credible. Don't try and do anything too arty; it's best to have a good face-to-camera shot, and make sure you are smiling! If you have products to promote, always ensure you have a good product shot against a white background.

Make sure you have high resolution images, as many publications need them. Also, images that are on a white background, so that publications can 'cut you out' against text.

Seventy percent of success in life

is showing up.

Woody Allen

STEP 5 - CLAIM YOUR NEW PLATFORM AND MAXIMISE YOUR VISIBILITY

Once you've discovered the skills into a new way forward, it's important to focus on the best way for you to get started to let everyone see at a glance the passion and authority you have around you, to revel in a new confidence to succeed, and to put into action the routes, paths and skills to get your message out there.

Ask yourself, "Where to next?" Ask, "Who do I need to be? What do I need to know? What do I need to do to get me there?" It's time to set the path of your 'passion profession' towards BIG CHANGES. You're ready to break out and play full out to take you and your authentic business to the next level.

I'd suggest getting clear on your personalised action plan or strategy to get yourself aligned and ready to manifest the leap forward, purposefully and passionately into a new era of your professional life. It may be that you need a team around you. It's brilliant to have support, and even if you aren't at the stage where you can pay full-time salaries, there's often an opportunity to hire virtual assistants, or to swap skills and time with friends who can do a job you need doing and you know you have something to offer back. You'll need to link up with the journalists/producers/bookers that could connect you to your ideal potential clients.

Invest some time in preparing a 'script' for each different situation so that you know exactly what to write or say to get your foot in the door.

I've stressed the importance of content, but your website is perhaps the most important content you may need to address. A winning website will keep the media, clients and potential clients interested and locked in to your passion and professionalism. Make sure you get the balance right; it's great having an all-singing, all-dancing website, but ultimately what the potential client wants to know is, am I in the right place? Could I like, know and trust this person? What can they do for me?

Remember that your website is your 'shop window'. Often, web developers, and the brand owner giving them their brief, get carried away with gorgeous pictures and moving images, but while your design must be congruent and eye-catching, the most important thing is that people know instantly that they are going to want to 'come inside'. There's a subconscious five-second test when arriving on a website for the first time. Try it yourself — land on a website of a brand whose product or service you may be interested in purchasing or finding out more about. Initially, you need to know you are in the right place. If it's a person you will be potentially working with, you will need to see them, to know that you can 'like, know and trust them'. Your subconscious mind will need to know that there is a strong brand message and that others value the service too. Once the five seconds of subconscious 'inner talk' has ceased, the potential buyer is fully engaged and can then start looking into other content. It's rather like making the decision to enter a store after something in the shop window has attracted you; once inside, you will take time to browse around — shopkeepers all know the important bit is getting customers in!

Even if you currently run a practice or any kind of business that relies on your hourly rate, it's worth considering the possibilities of 'earning while you sleep' because you could radically maximise the leverage of your time, energy and business. One well-known entrepreneur has a programme that makes a cash register *'ker-ching'* sound every time anything is bought from her website – very cool!

As a fellow small business owner, author, expert and teacher, I fully recognise that conventional business training and marketing practices don't always appeal to those who have a heart-centred business, but there is lots of help available. Find someone to work with who is a good few steps ahead of you. I've developed what I hope is a very special holistic-focused training, which can help you to find conscious approaches to achieving the visibility and success that you deserve.

Whether you're starting a new business, are self-employed, or even if you are someone (or a company) who already has your own external PR for your product or services, recognise if you need help and find someone who can show you how to maximise your own personal profile, how to publicise yourself and your business in a multitude of ways and how to get your message out there. You then become your own best advertisement for your business. You are the brand.

The caterpillar does all the work,
but the butterfly gets all
the publicity.

George Carlin

CHECKLIST FOR A 'PR-READY' MEDIA KIT

It's a good idea to have collated all your promotional materials to attract attention for your business into one well-organised 'packet' or electronic file that can be delivered digitally (you may also want to have physical copies for direct marketing, but always have a digital version available).

This compendium of information is sometimes called your 'Media Kit', and is how you will make your first impression. Here's a checklist to ensure that you are PR/media-ready. Sometimes you may only need to send a journalist or a producer an email with one short paragraph; they will contact you if they want more, so you need to be sure it's all ready to go. Your media kit may be as simple as a series of digital documents and images, or it might be more elaborate and include glossy printed documents, brochures, CDs, and more. However simplistic your media kit, keep the design cohesive so that there is clarity around you and your brand. Everything listed here won't necessarily apply to your business, but in general you will need:

- **A brand name/brand logo.** ☐

- **'Mission statement' or tag line** that describes you or ☐ your business.

- **Introductory email or letter.** Have a pre-written version ☐ of this ready to go; of course, you can personalise it each time you send. This is your 'pitch' that will hopefully encourage the reader to want to know more.

It will include your 'mission statement' or tag line that describes you or your business. The header should include your brand name and logo. Always ensure you include contact information.

- **Press release(s).** ☐

  This is a 'release to the press' to inform of new products or services, or to promote an event aimed directly at journalists editors and producers. NB: This is not the same as a sales flyer for customers. Ensure that your press release tells the full story of what's new in the first paragraph. Include an image and any embargo dates, in the 'Notes to Editors' section, and include all contact information and links to where more images, biogs etc. can be accessed.

  Important tip: If you are hoping that a journalist will use your information, remember they may simply want to cut and paste part of the material, so don't send it as a PDF; send as a Microsoft Word document.

- **Company/Brand biog.** ☐

  Even if you are a solopreneur or sole trader, do note this is not a CV. A company biog should include the history of the brand, and its core values, ethics and objectives. This is a good place to include any awards, achievements and forthcoming plans. Include information about the key players in the business.

- **Social media and analytics.**
  If your brand is successful on social media, it would be good to give evidence of your influence and social media reach. You could include details of the platforms used, your followers, blog stats, if appropriate, growth profile and google analytics.

- **Products/services information.**
  If you sell products, you may wish to outline your main USP here, the benefits of the products, ingredients where appropriate, and client reviews or testimonials. If you are a service provider, outline your main offers, and provide case studies or testimonials from clients. You could also include a list of Frequently Asked Questions about your brand. If you have lots of products and information, create single sheets for ease of use.

- **Press coverage.**
  If you have been featured in any magazines or articles, you may want to include the coverage in this section. Do bear in mind though, if you are trying to attract coverage in a specific publication, they may decide not to feature you if they are reminded that you have had press exposure in competitive publications!

- **Multimedia.**
  If you are hoping to be featured on TV or radio in any form, then editors and producers will want to see you in action and hear your voice. Include links to recordings, podcasts and videos you have been featured in or demos

you have created specifically to showcase yourself and your work/products.

- **Images and logos.** ☐
  A publication may want to reproduce your logo and images of you and your products. Don't clog up their inbox with the actual images, but if relevant send a thumbnail image and make it clear that they can request high resolution versions from you. It may be easier to have an 'images kit' on your website so that you can give a link where journalists can download the images they need.

  Important tip: Ideally you will need professional photographs of you against a white background, and the same applies to products. Journalists will want to use a 'cut-out' of the product so don't only have a photograph of your product against your logo or against a coloured background.

Remember to update your media kit regularly.

EXERCISES AND ASSIGNMENTS

Here's a 'Mini Programme' for you to try out a few exercises. It should help give you some ideas as to how you can move forward.

The exercises and assignments are going to be centred around defining your brand and identifying your ideal clients and the best way to reach them through your PR and marketing. Remember the importance of content writing, strategies for social media, approaching journalists and issuing press releases.

Of course, everyone works at their own pace, but if you are just building your business and brand, then it's very useful to give yourself the deadlines of needing to complete this work within a specific time frame. I'd suggest around six weeks. I'm guessing, all things being equal, you are also working or running your business! It's worth noting though that most journalists and editors issue requests for help with articles and opportunities for you with about 12 to 24 hours' notice, sometimes less, so having the skills up your sleeve of being able to personalise some text that's perhaps been prepared in advance will stand you in good stead. It's worth committing a few hours over two or three days each week to complete this initial work.

The great thing about these exercises, by the way, is that in many cases, you are creating content that you can use right away to start promoting yourself, so it's not just wasted time. If writing is just not your thing yet, then do the written assignments as an audio recording, or even a mini video clip.

EXERCISE 1 - BRAND VISUALISATION

The very first exercise that I'd like you to do may well be out of your comfort zone, but it's worth doing it anyway. I've worked with people who have amazing creative insights from this one short exercise.

YOU IN THE SPOTLIGHT – A SHORT VISUALISATION

For anyone who may be thinking, "Whoooa, hold on... I thought this was a book full of practical tips on building my writing and content preparation skills and techniques, and getting visibility for my brand and business, not some floaty pseudo spiritual claptrap," don't panic. It absolutely is, but I do believe in the holistic approach in business and that means the whole mind, body and spirit – it's all connected. If you haven't yet made the connection between your subconscious mind and what happens in your life, then you're going to be in for a treat. This visualisation is going to be a very exciting way for you to get in touch with your subconscious mind; it will hopefully give you new insights into you as a brand, your USP, and your ideal clients.

I'm going to keep this explanation very short because I'm guessing for most of you, connecting with your spirituality and getting in touch with the deeper part of who you are is very much part of your everyday life. In case you are new to it, I'd just like to strongly recommend you to keep an open mind. Try doing this guided visualisation and just see what comes up for you as you start to really become aware of the importance of what's going on with you, spiritually and emotionally, and how that will affect your success in your career and in business.

Your subconscious mind is incredibly powerful and yet it's just that, subconscious, buried deep down. If we can connect with it and even reprogramme it, we can literally change our thought patterns and **what we attract to us**. It's like changing our DNA, but to change it, you need to first be aware of it, and tap into how it functions. What's quite profound, I think, is just how huge our subconscious mind is compared to our conscious mind.

It's worth remembering that the subconscious part of who we are is rather like a hard drive on a computer; it carries all our knowledge, beliefs and thoughts, and yet it has no power of reason or judgement. It doesn't usually differentiate between what's true and what isn't. It's a cool analogy to think of your subconscious mind as one big Google search engine! If you have the belief that clients can't afford to come to you and you moan to friends and family that hardly anyone ever calls to book an appointment, then your subconscious mind acts as if you have typed into the search box, *'I don't get many paying clients,'* and it will find ways to deliver that truth to you.

Alternatively, if you say out loud, **"I am attracting lots of perfect clients who really want and need my service,"** your little subconscious internal 'Google spiders' will go off and seek out ways of making that come true for you. I know that this feels just too simplistic for some people, they simply don't believe that just by wanting – or as some call it, 'cosmically ordering' – something that it will be yours for the asking, but if you are sceptical, I strongly recommend you do further research on this widely documented topic and try this for yourselves. If you're starting to wonder, "What the heck has this got to do with me PR-ing my business?" Well, *more than you may think*! If you are new to the concept of the power of the subconscious mind, just try taking yourself on a journey now and see what pops up to the surface; sometimes it can be surprising.

So let's get ready to do this very powerful visualisation. It's written below, so you can read it first, then close your eyes and remember what to look out for. For far more power, you can download the guided visualisation from *www.janeyleegrace.com/resources*

You will need a piece of paper and a pen or pencil ready to hand for afterwards, and I'd hope that you are somewhere where you can get comfortable, you won't be disturbed and there aren't too many distractions. Obviously it's not appropriate to listen to the recording while driving or operating machinery, as it's a closed eye experience.

If listening to the audio isn't appropriate for you, here's the content written out. If you prefer, you can record it in your own voice.

VISUALISATION – YOU IN THE SPOTLIGHT

Gather your pen and paper and put it to one side and sit as comfortably as possible, but with a straight back. Uncross your legs and just have your hands resting in your lap. If you are feeling a little apprehensive about this, please don't feel concerned; it's not hypnosis, you can resume normal procedures at any time, and you will be awake and alert at any time you need to be. Don't feel you have to share any of the thoughts that come to you either; this is for you alone and what comes to mind will usually be from a deeper part of your being. It's a good idea not to try and rationalise it too much as you go along or be too judgemental; just for once switch off the super ego and tap into a different part of you.

Set an intention that you will be able to relax deeply but that you will stay awake and will be able to remember everything that happens during the closed eye process in order to benefit from it.

Settle into a comfortable seated position, close your eyes and take deep breaths, in through your nose and out through your mouth. Now do that again, and as you exhale, imagine that you are relaxing and sinking deeper and deeper. In your own time, take seven deep breaths, in through the nose and out through the mouth, and with each exhalation, imagine you are going deeper and deeper into relaxation. You are becoming calmer, everything is slowing down. With your eyes closed, imagine that you can see yourself; you are both experiencing and observing yourself, noticing your thoughts and feelings.

Take yourself for a walk. You can choose if you are walking through fields or along the beach, but notice your surroundings. Is the sun shining? Is there a breeze? You feel at peace, easy and relaxed, walking and feeling good. Now I want to imagine you are beamed from wherever you've been enjoying your leisurely walk into a town or city centre; you are now walking along a busy street. Imagine the shops and buildings as you pass by; you can be anywhere in the world. Take a moment to see if you can identify where you're walking; taking jaunty steps. You can both experience yourself walking along and see yourself as if watching another person.

As you walk along, experience other people jostling you as they pass by; is it daytime or night-time? After a little while, you come to a street corner. You turn to the left, and as you do, there ahead of you is a huge advertising billboard. You stop in your tracks; the billboard is advertising your brand. Take a moment to notice what it's an advertisement for; is it for a book, products, a store, a TV series, movie, a live event? Is there an image of you? If so, how do you look? What does the text say? What's the overall feel of the brand that is being promoted?

As you get closer, you see a whole group of people gathering around the billboard. They are very interested in what it says. Some are chatting to each other about it. Have a look at these people and notice something about them; are they men or women? What age? How are they dressed? Can you hear what they are saying?

Have another good look at that advertising hoarding and set the intention you will recall all your first thoughts about it. Now turn another corner, and as if by magic (it's fine if you've had to be beamed to another country), you are now standing outside your own business premises, whether that be your home, a factory unit, rented clinic space, whatever. You are pleased to be invisible because as you reach the entrance, you see a client walking out speaking on a mobile phone. He or she is relating details of the experience they have just had, speaking in quite an animated way about you, your brand, service, what you have just done for them. Listen carefully to what they are saying. PAUSE... Now, take a deep breath and slowly bring yourself back into the now, breathing normally. Just take a few moments to jot down what came to mind; if literally nothing came up for you, don't panic; you will have this recording to do at another time, perhaps when you are more relaxed and in the zone. It's fine to do it again, but of course, it's not quite as powerful as the first time because your subconscious mind knows what's coming. Nevertheless, if you open yourself to what your subconscious mind has in store for you, I'm convinced you will get an insight.

I hope that was powerful for some of you. One woman I did this exercise with saw herself in New York's Times Square and the billboard was advertising a huge live event that she has since started plotting and planning. It's all coming to fruition, so powerful things can happen when you get in touch with your deepest desires and what you really want.

If that worked for you, why not try the visualisation around confidence being a public speaker? You can find this on the same link at *www.janeyleegrace.com/resources*

VISUALISATION – YOU ON THE STAGE

Settle down into a comfortable position. Have a pen and paper to hand. This visualisation will get you in touch with you as a confident public speaker, and I hope that applies to you because even if you don't intend to become a speaker, you may be asked to give a short presentation or speech, so these skills will be invaluable.

Close your eyes and take a deep breath, slowly calm your breathing down. Start to take yourself on a journey. You are arriving at a building where you are booked to give a talk, or a presentation or speech. As you arrive at the entrance, notice where you are. Is it a conference? A theatre or school building? Perhaps a community centre or village hall? You enter and there on a noticeboard, or a welcoming lectern, is your name. See your name written there, against the time you are speaking. You are met by the event organiser, who gives you a warm welcome and tells you the audience is very much looking forward to your appearance.

The organiser takes you to a side room, or backstage if it's a theatre, and tells you that you have ten 10 minutes until you are on. You become aware of the speaker who is currently talking to the audience; his or her talk seems to be going well. You stand and breathe. You choose one of the confidence techniques you have researched, such as choosing a trigger memory, a memory of a time when you felt totally fantastic and full of confidence. Bring back that feeling and breathe deeply and say to yourself, and your subconscious mind, "I am a confident and powerful public speaker, I am authentic and have a unique message to share." You feel your feet firmly rooted, you feel grounded, enough oxygen, fully prepared. You have just the right amount of adrenaline flowing, so you have enough nerves to feel energy and at the top of your game, but not enough to inhibit you. You glance at your notes written on cards but you feel fully confident that you won't need to use them. The three sections of your talk are already embedded deeply, you feel as though you ARE your message, you embody what it is you want to share.

The organiser comes back and says, "Two minutes." You feel a flutter of nerves, but you calm the inner talk. The organiser goes onto the stage area and thanks the previous speaker, and gives a wonderful introduction to you. You hear your own potted biography; it sounds good. "Please welcome here today..." and the organiser says your name. As you step forward, the audience burst into applause.

You get to the stage and stand with your feet just slightly apart and you drink in these wonderful people; they are smiling expectantly at you, keen to hear your message. You begin your talk with your intriguing, amusing or entertaining story or intro to kick it off. From the moment you start speaking, you sense that this is going brilliantly, the audience love you; they smile and laugh in the right places, or look concerned when the information is shocking or serious. You flow easily from your introduction into the main themes of your talk and then build to a crescendo where you give them some really powerful information or ask a very provocative question. You pause there for effect... and then smoothly start to conclude and summarise. Your conclusion leaves them feeling inspired to change. You deliver your final words, say thank you and they burst intro rapturous applause. You step away from the stage and punch the air as you get back into the backstage area. Yes, you rocked it!

People are queuing to talk to you and learn more from you, and this is just the beginning of more events for you, where you can share your knowledge and expertise.

Slowly come back to the present moment and take a few seconds to jot down any of the first thoughts that came to mind. Don't worry if you saw nothing; you can sample it again at another time.

EXERCISE 2 - CORE VALUES

G et clarity on your values, especially as to how they relate to your key messages.

Here's some suggestions of words, in no particular order, that are often used in leadership and personal development training. This list is by no means extensive. Add lots of your own; these are just to give some ideas. Try and add at least 25 more words to this list before you start the exercise.

Abundance Bliss Artistic Gratitude Facilitate Family Radiance Happiness Intuitive Enjoyment Dedication Spirit Attractive Direction Peace Mastery Creativity Movement Encourage Vibrant Integration Discerning Awareness Investigate Caring Wealth Coach Adventurous Patience Compassion Articulate Leadership Fun Freedom Resilience Enlighten Energy Influence Sexual Community Inspiration Teacher Unique inspiration Greatness Honour Passionate Investigate Uplifting Integrity Health Inspiration Confidence Original Beauty Truth Standards Kindness Detox Brilliance Responsive Belonging Imagination Transformational Prayer Control Diversity Content Capable Perception Courage Dreamlike Understanding Design Emotion Grace Excellence Enjoyment Glamour Influence

Once you have an extensive list of words, look at the ones that stand out; words that express qualities, terms and concepts that are of value to you, that are of utmost importance in your life.

You can do this exercise both generally and specifically, i.e. how your values relate to your work, and how you are perceived when you are 'in the spotlight'. For example, if you are doing this exercise for your life as a whole and you have a family, one of your top core values might be 'Fun', but you may not necessarily feel that this a core value for your work, especially if your key message is one of a serious nature. Your core values around how to promote your work to others may focus on different values altogether.

Initially, you may look at all the 'positive' words and think you would want them all, but ultimately being in touch with which values are at the core of you, the ones that are critical for you to feel comfortable and authentic, is essential as it will enable you to make the right decisions consistently.

<u>Once you have defined your core values, it's time to prioritise</u>

- Circle 20 words that are intrinsically your core values (in relation to getting your message out to a wider audience)
- Then reduce the list to 10
- Finally, reduce it down to 5
- Rank the top 5 core values in order of importance for you right now (mark them A to E with A being the number one core value).

Against each core value, rank them as to how you are doing right now. If there is a difference between what think is important and what you are currently focusing on, then you will need to do some adjusting! Sometimes it can come as a surprise that what's most important to you is not at the forefront of your mind.

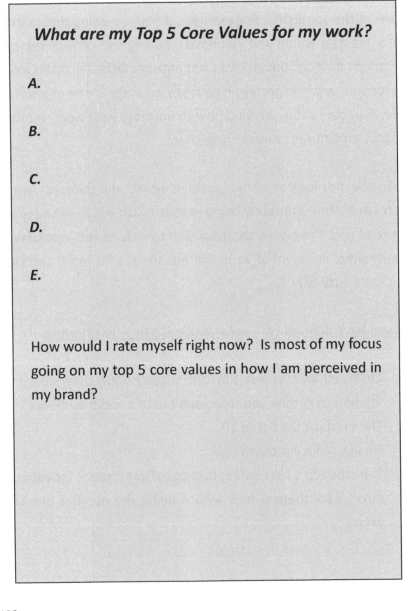

What are my Top 5 Core Values for my work?

A.

B.

C.

D.

E.

How would I rate myself right now? Is most of my focus going on my top 5 core values in how I am perceived in my brand?

EXERCISE 3 - CHOOSE YOUR TRIBE

Your visualisation may have helped you with identifying your ideal client, or you may already have clarity in this, but it's worth getting in touch with your ideal client and what their needs are. Ask yourself, *"Who is it that I want to serve?"*

You may decide to create a client avatar, invent a fictional character, build a photo online for him or her, and write a one page profile. This could include where they work, how much they earn, what their relationships are like, what they do in their spare time, what problems they may have in their life, where they like to hang out socially, what websites they are likely to frequent, and what social networks they use most.

Try and imagine someone who is the perfect client for you. If creating a fictional avatar doesn't resonate, choose a real person, someone you know a little, but not too well. Write their name on a piece of paper. Now, imagine what the various aspects of their life might be like (it doesn't matter if you don't get this right, it's just an imaginative exercise) and what their key problems might be in relation to the solutions you could provide.

For example, if you are a massage therapist, you may imagine your ideal client as a busy, stressed working mother. You imagine that she is busy rushing around and rarely gets time to look after herself, so perhaps she is feeling stressed, a little burnt out. Does she have backache and shoulder pain? Is she likely to be using Facebook asking for recommendations? Is there a health centre in your locality that she may frequent? Would she read the local press?

Try and get into her thought process and come up with five issues that are important to her.

When you have decided upon five 'problems' or issues that your ideal client has and have written them down, write down the solution to that problem that you feel confident that you can provide. The five 'step' system could become your 'signature system' that offers the solutions you can provide, and could even create the framework for blogs, articles, eBooks, or even online programmes.

EXERCISE 4 - SING YOUR OWN PRAISES – YOUR YOU-NIQUE BRILLIANCE

Draw a heart or a symbol in the centre of the page. Write your own name inside it and then, at any place around it, create something between a mind map and a vision board as you write down all your best qualities and achievements. This is where you write down everything you are good at; there's no room for modesty here!

Ask yourself the questions outlined below and be as emotive as you like! You should end up with a piece of paper that has on it lots of wonderful superlative words and phrases such as, 'I am enthusiastic and trustworthy,' 'I have healing hands,' 'I'm intuitive,' and longer phrases such as, 'I'm the catalyst for change...' or, 'I'm full of innovative ideas...' You must also throw in personal achievements or even something quirky such as, 'I make a great apple pie,' or in my case, 'I can find amazing retro clothes in charity shops.' This helps you determine your own USP, what is unique about you. It helps you to define your brand promise. Using your coloured pencils, get creative and draw some images that represent any of the things you have mentioned. This is not about creating a work of art, more about allowing your subconscious mind to create a visual representative of your unique brilliance.

- What are my best skills and talents?
- What do others appreciate in me?
- How do I inspire/encourage/empower others?
- Why should someone buy my product/service?

- Why should I be called upon to be the expert in my field?
- What is my brand promise?

It's worth noting that many people find the 'professional achievements' part of this exercise relatively easy to do, but it gets trickier when they add in the personal bits. Most commonly, clients write phrases to describe their You-nique brilliance such as, 'Good listener,' 'Great at transforming others,' 'Good leadership skills,' 'Professional,' 'Authentic,' ... I usually then ask them to remember back to what we discussed about the importance of people doing business with those they like, know and trust. Remember we said we could all go to any dentist in any town, but we don't, do we?

If I was seeking to find a life coach, for example, I would expect someone who is a 'good listener' and is 'professional and authentic' to be prerequisite skills and traits. It's the more personal stuff that determines whether I am drawn to them, whether I can like, know and trust them. Are they traditional, quirky, and humorous? Can they make an incredible apple pie, and dance salsa? One successful business woman I worked with simply couldn't think of anything at all to draw or write. Eventually, I asked her in desperation, "Did you ever run a marathon? Pass your driving test first time? Get a swimming certificate or swim the channel?" At the mention of the word 'swim', her eyes lit up and suddenly she started enthusing about her distant hobby of snorkelling and swimming. She told me some fascinating stories about what's under the sea and even joked that she felt perhaps she was a mermaid...

I asked her to add it loud and proud to the 'You-nique brilliance' vision board, and as she did, some wonderful colourful images emerged. It didn't take too much to see how she had never thought to integrate this important part of who she was into her business life. When she began to see the connection, she was able to rekindle her passion for her products and her marketing, and indeed went on to seemingly effortlessly create a whole new brand and profile called 'The Authentic Mermaid'.

Another woman I worked with found the 'missing part' of herself was her humour and ability to make people laugh. Within weeks, her client list had trebled as she started offering humorous yet insightful blogs and social media messages. People loved her sense of fun, which had somehow been missing from her work, yet was such a strong USP. She integrated her YOU-nique brilliance.

Take your time over this exercise. Once you have written down all the important words and phrases that feel important, and drawn some images to represent them, look again to see if there are ways to integrate some of the 'personal', even perhaps forgotten, parts of you into the work that you do. Of course, I am not suggesting that everything that feels important here will feature in your marketing, or will even necessarily be added to the 'About me' section of your website, but I would recommend that you remind yourself of its importance. Often the things that we're good at and really enjoyed before we started our business have been buried, and yet have great importance – even if only to provide some fun! In any case, consider reconnecting with those parts of you that you may have forgotten. That long forgotten talent of songwriting, or that ability to lift weights despite being tiny, could be one of the many facets that make up who you are, that make you unique, and once you have identified these facets, these interests, skills or talents, there's just a possibility that they can be used in all manner of ways to relate to ideal clients, directly or indirectly.

In any case, I never find people feel it was a waste of time. It's always worthwhile remembering what's special about you and what makes you different from other successful people in your arena.

EXERCISE 5 - YOU AND YOUR BRAND VISION BOARD

Ensure that you won't be disturbed (you'll be amazed how absorbed in this task you will become) and spread everything out around you. Open up some magazines or newspapers, and cut out anything that seems to represent your future business plans, profile or personal life. (It can be a good idea to do a separate vison board for a specific business goal or project.) It might be a collection of letters, words, phrases or images, both in colour and black and white. When you have a huge pile, start creating a vision board. Literally glue the cuttings on in whatever order seems to feel right, overlapping if you choose. It's a great idea to just 'feel' into this exercise; add anything you want, using a pen or crayons, and intuitively create an amazing vision of your future. Your vision board should end up looking like an exciting colourful collection of optimistic phrases, words, pictures, bits of fabric, stickers and symbols that represent success, happiness and wealth, for both your personal and professional life.

Something magical can happen with vision boards; it's well documented that opportunities are created which marry completely with the images visualised. One colleague of mine travelled a lot and kept her version of a vision board in a beautiful leather-bound book. She added pages as she went along, and now she often marvels and looks back at those images and dreams collected on her travels. She now lives and works in her ultimate dream profession in exactly the place she had cut out an image of from a magazine years ago. She just thought the coastline looked beautiful so she stuck it in her vision book. When she later created an opportunity for herself, it turned out to be in the magical place Deia, Mallorca. She had no idea it even existed; it turned out to be the exact coastline she had represented on her vision board.

Be careful what you dream of; your dreams might come true. My children are quite excited about this, as I recently did a new vision board and, in my almost hypnotic state as I sat cutting and pasting from magazines, I found I had added a picture of a gorgeous scruffy mongrel dog. I definitely don't have time for a pet in my life and, despite my children's protests, that wasn't going to change. The children's hopes were risen again when they saw the image and I found myself slightly panicky that somehow I would end up with a dog – bizarrely, I was secretly wishing my wish wouldn't come true! The universe, however, delivered this particular subconscious wish in a most innovative way.

A few weeks after I had created my board, a neighbour knocked on our door with a lovely new puppy in her arms. Yes, you've guessed it, the exact gorgeous scruffy mongrel. "I want to introduce you to my new dog," she said beaming. "I hoped your children might like to walk him from time to time?" Result! All the joy of a dog with none of the responsibility!

EXERCISE 6 - WRITE A FEATURE ARTICLE ABOUT YOURSELF

This is your story, but it's not the same as a biography or CV. It shouldn't include boring factual stuff, but it should include anything of interest, whether personal or professional, that readers may find captivating and inspiring.

Imagine it as a profile piece written in a magazine. Have a look at one of the Sunday supplements. Imagine there's a feature about successful leaders or entrepreneurs in your type of business. There are five or six different professionals profiled there, and yours is one of the profile pieces. Three hundred words; that's all you have to sell yourself and capture the attention of potential ideal clients. Remember that the reader will want to learn something about you. What makes you tick? What was the pivotal moment that made you who you are today, that resulted in you doing the work that you are now doing? In crafting this story, do so with your ideal client in mind as the reader; what would they want to know about you? Probably how many qualifications you got at school wouldn't be of interest, but the fact that you found your new year's resolutions list from when you were 11 years old which stated, 'I will give up sugar and chocolate,' might be of interest if you are now a healthy eating specialist.

Anything dramatic or impressive that has happened in your life is bound to have made an impact on who you are today, so despite the fact that you may not feel it is relevant to your business, ask yourself whether it makes interesting reading in connection with your work. If this flows easily for you, in addition write a short biog too. Most journalists will require this if they are to write about you. Aim for 100 words, then 50. You may find the less words you have to play with, the harder it is! Be sure to include your website URL in any bio you write.

EXERCISE 7 - CREATE A PERSONAL PROFILE Q & A

You may have seen these in magazines; they're usually fairly light-hearted quick-fire questions. Often the subject is a celebrity or a politician, someone in the public eye, but it's a nice way of sharing some info about yourself, and there's no reason why you can't pop your own profile piece on your website or blog. Don't just answer the questions factually; think about them long enough to create an interesting article.

This is a fun exercise that isn't requiring any literary skill. It is simply offering the relevant bits of info that you know will be of interest to your ideal clients. It's a nice way of showing them that you are not so very different from them, but you may have the solution to their problem! It's the beginning of the 'like, know and trust' approach. If it's appropriate, change the questions to suit what it is you'd like to get across.

A Minute or Two with Julie XYZ from XYZ and Co.

- Who is the face behind the label?

- What's your USP?

- What time does your typical day start?

- Full English or yoghurt and muesli?

- What drives you?

- What are you most proud of in your business?

- What bit of advice would you give to your younger self starting out?

- What brings you to be doing what you're doing today?

- If you could be Prime Minister for a day, what one thing would you do?

- Tell us one very quirky thing about you.

- Go on sing your praises; show off about anything you like!

- Perfectionist or bodger?

- If your business was a song, what would it be?

- What would you like people to say about your brand when they recommend to friends?

...you get the idea!

EXERCISE 8 - CREATE AND FINE-TUNE YOUR PERSONAL BRAND MESSAGES

Hopefully you have developed some clarity on who you are and what you are a stand for. It's also a great idea to be clear on your core values and your purpose.

I'd urge you to create a statement that describes who you are and what you do; it needs to be powerful, focused and clear, and should appeal to your ideal clients and potential customers. It can include your purpose (sometimes called a 'mission statement') and can work really well placed right at the top of your website, especially if you are a key person of influence.

From these statements, you may also craft a 'brand mantra', a short powerful memorable phrase that should be seven words or less (usually for your personal use to keep you motivated and 'on message'.

Similarly, you can come up with a 'tag line' which communicates the essence of your brand to potential customers; again, ideally it will be a maximum seven words.

You may also want to think of one word that sums up You and all you do – beware this can be tricky!

'ELEVATOR PITCH'

Your elevator pitch is a very short summary of what you do, or what you create, as well as who your target market is and what the problem is that your product solves. Also define what the strong USP is that would make the person in the elevator intrigued to know more so that they ask for your business card before stepping out. It wouldn't actually be possible to pitch the sum total of your work in a few seconds, but if you get your 'one liner' pitch right, you can invoke enough intrigue or interest that the person listening will know that they want to hear more.

It's likely you will need several attempts at this. Often, we are so close to what we do that we can't come up with a succinct description of what our own service is, or how our product affects change. By working through this one, it will help to give you clarity. This will also be beneficial later when preparing for radio/TV interviews etc.

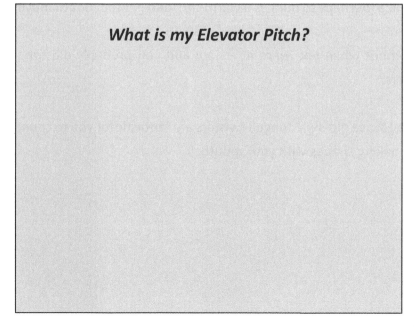

What is my Elevator Pitch?

BONUS EXERCISE - VOICE TECHNIQUE TONGUE TWISTERS

Our voice is an instrument, a wind instrument, and we need to look after it. Most of you aren't aiming to be singers, but warming up the voice, and recognising it and honouring it, is still important if it is to support you in a situation where you are nervous. Breathing properly and preparing your mouth, literally using the vocal chords before you 'perform', whether that be for a presentation or for an interview, is crucial.

Get into the habit of noticing your stretching, vocalising, breathing, and posture.

Ideally, you would stretch out the body, remember your posture, use the voice (perhaps to hum as a warm-up), and get the mouth moving.

Remember when you were at school and you probably did tongue twisters?

Well all those old-style tongue twisters are fantastic for you to connect with making shapes with your mouth.

TONGUE TWISTERS

The tip of the tongue, the teeth, and the lips.

―――――――

She sells sea shells on the sea shore.

―――――――

A box of biscuits,
a box of mixed biscuits,
and a biscuit mixer.

―――――――

Sister Susie went to sea
to see the sea, you see.
The sea she saw was a saucy sea,
a sort of saucy sea saw she.

―――――――

Better Botter bought some butter.
"But," she said, "this butter's bitter!
If I put it in my batter,
it will make my batter bitter."
So she bought some better butter,
put it in her bitter batter,
and it made her bitter batter better.

———————

When tweedle beetles battle,
with paddles in a puddle,
they call it a tweedle beetle puddle paddle battle.
Dr. Seuss

———————

Have fun with tongue twisters, and perhaps make up your own.

SUCCESS STORIES

Here's a selection of success stories. These are the stories of people I have worked with, people who I have coached or who did the masterclass programme, and what effect it had on their businesses. I won't apologise for the fact that they're glowing testimonials for me too, but I hope from these personal accounts, you will gain some insights and take to heart the power that these approaches can have in real situations. I hope they will inspire you to put yourself into your brand!

Information about the programmes / audios / coaching these entrepreneurs refer to can be found at www.janeyleegrace.com

SHANN'S STORY

We milk our pedigree goats on our family smallholding in Wales, and use their raw milk to handcraft probiotic kefir, and kefir skincare that is healing for eczema, rosacea and psoriasis. All of our products are made by hand on the farm, and are completely free from any artificial dyes, perfumes, phthalates, parabens or petrochemicals.

We only began trading three years ago, so our visibility was zero. I have a background in the media so I knew that good PR was essential if we were going to get our business off the ground. I was referred to Janey Lee Grace's website through a contact, and was impressed at the comprehensiveness of her grasp on the natural product field.

Janey advised me to put my face on the business, as people will buy from someone they know, like and trust. So I started doing that. I got very active with creating press releases, and getting the news out there. And the biggest thing – she really pushed me to write a book, self-published. I did this, and the book has since been picked up by Hay House, for release in February 2015. My book became an Amazon No 1 bestseller, which has been a lifelong dream for me. It never would have happened if Janey hadn't pushed me to write the book to begin with.

Life took a strange turn when my husband Rich came out of hospital infected with antibiotic-resistant MRSA. The doctors couldn't help us, and we feared for his life. Desperate, I researched until I found an ancient black plague remedy using essential oils. I mixed my own version of this, used it on Rich along with medical honey and our own probiotic kefir – and it worked. Rich swabbed completely clear of MRSA two weeks later.

Janey then helped us leverage this dramatic backstory into a series of high-level editorial stories in national publications, including *The Sun*, *Woman's Own*, *Country Smallholding Magazine*, etc. Our budget for paid advertising is zero – we spend all of our current marketing budget with Janey, and the amount of editorial publicity that she creates for us has driven our growth.

We saw even more growth. We were shortlisted in the FreeFrom SkinCare Awards. Editorial articles about us were published in numerous newspaper and magazines. We secured TV and radio pieces. We had a big article in the *Daily Mail YOU Magazine* which led to a slot on the Steve Wright show on Radio Two. We were then filmed by ITV's *Countrywise*. We had so many orders that our website crashed. We went from one employee to 12 full-time team members in the space of one year, and are currently projected to turn over more than one million pounds next year. All of this, and we do no paid advertising!

We also collaborated with the Innovation Sector of the Welsh Assembly Government and Aberystwyth University research scientists, and achieved the Investors in People Award. We're very proud of how far our little company has come.

Shann Jones

MARIAN'S STORY

I started an organic skincare business by accident! I've worked in the field of complementary health for nearly 20 years as a Kinesiologist, Craniosacral therapist and Nutritionist. One summer evening, a client was lying on my treatment table complaining that she couldn't find any moisturisers she could use; everything she tried made her skin feel itchy or she came out in a rash. I asked if I could make a moisturiser for her, and as I'm a Kinesiologist, I was able to test the ingredients she couldn't have. I made a cream which she loved and she then asked me to make more creams for her six sisters in Ireland as Christmas presents. Happily, they loved the creams and asked if I could make more.

I started selling creams to clients in my practice, and very soon I had a light bulb moment where I saw that I could infuse the creams with the healing properties of homoeopathic remedies and flower essences. Having worked with energy medicine in my practice for many years, I knew that I could apply the same principles of using 'energy' to my products.

The feedback was very good. People said they really made a difference so I took the decision to make them available to everyone, not just clients in my practice. Celgenics was born!

I quickly realised that as the new girl on the block, a newcomer to the world of beauty and cosmetics, I needed publicity. My first foray into hiring someone was a disaster. The person concerned promised much, and delivered little.

My next experience was altogether different and I worked with a lovely team of girls who were genuinely interested in what I did and secured mentions for me in various magazines.

The idea of getting some training myself on how to do PR seemed too good to miss, so I signed up for an online series of Masterclass training webinars with Janey Lee Grace. One of the things I realised in working with the PR companies was that it was me who did most of the work in terms of putting together the right information to go out. I then paid them to find the right people to talk to!

Out of her training, I created press releases so that I then had to hand when a press request came in. Usually press requests seem to arrive in one's inbox with about 24 hours' notice. To create a press release from scratch just isn't feasible with such short notice, so it was really useful to be prepared in advance. Sometimes a press release needs tweaking to fit the particular request, but it's generally a very quick and easy thing to do.

As a result of having these press releases prepared in advance, I've been able to use them on a number of different occasions, resulting in a couple of quite lengthy press releases which has been great to boost the profile of Celgenics.

Putting a video on my website was also great advice, and making the website much more personalised was an excellent learning – as Janey says, 'people buy from people' and what better way for people to learn about you and what you do from a video. Most of my PR activities have been responding to press requests but I also had great success in going out and inviting journalists and bloggers to experience my Celenics Couture Antiageing Facial.

Promoting myself like this was helped, I'm sure, by Janey's advice on the course to get my message out there. I have a duty to be heard!

Marian Bourne

BARBARA'S STORY

I'm a raw food chef and rock singer! I specialise in creating delicious raw food recipes for time-challenged people, making multi-purpose meals to share with partners, friends or small children – all of which are ready in five minutes or less!

I provide online recipe books, food prep tips and coaching. I also sing about raw food through spoof songs where I take popular pop/rock songs and give them a healthy food twist.

A couple of years ago, I was just getting started with my blog. I have always been fascinated by advertising and PR from my years as a singer. I knew that a brand's strength and presence are very important, but I didn't know how to get my message out in the most effective way. I felt intimidated by contacting the media for some reason. Janey and I met at a business event two years ago, and when I heard Janey talk about her mission of helping heart-centred businesses, I knew she would be the perfect person to help me! To get started, I posted to my blog regularly and asked people what problems they wanted to solve, and what they wanted to know about raw food. I created a free gift on my website. My first photo – the most successful so far – has me only wearing cabbage (well, pinned to a bathing suit but no one has to know!) and sitting on a piano singing. Having an eye-catching photo that would stand out was important to me. Then I knew I needed to contact the media, which is where I needed help.

The only PR training I've ever had was with Janey on her Masterclass course, and I got absolutely loads out of it. Probably the best was Janey teaching us how to prepare for an interview: learning how to anticipate questions you might be asked, how to steer the interview along so that you can get your main point across, and how you can best contribute to what the journalist is looking for to serve his/her audience. Another great takeaway was an exercise that we did to come up with endless ideas for a book, for blog posts – for all kinds of content. I have all my course materials in a special binder and I refer to them still when preparing for PR activities today.

I loved Janey's enthusiasm, but also the sheer volume of practical tips. We did a visualisation where we saw ourselves on a huge billboard – and now I'm actually seeing that image in print, which is amazing!

The one thing I had no clue about was how to prepare what to say for an interview. I think without Janey's course, I would have just winged it, whereas now I prepare! Before Janey's course, I would have procrastinated like mad before contacting the media, but now I just dive in because as Janey says, journalists are just as much in need of a good story as we are in need of good publicity!

As a result of the coaching, I did all the homework! I created my own biogs – both long and short versions, as well as a huge mind map of main topics for my content. I created the full chapter outline of my first book, which I will start writing later this year, and I created my first press release and contacted some specialist publications.

I've contributed recipes and articles to specialist magazines, both online and offline. I use my spoof songs for live events for both online and offline publicity. I've done raw food demonstrations with free tastings. I'm currently preparing the launch of my new website and writing the promotional content for that, after which I'll start on my first book.

I saw a big increase in my subscriber list (200 to 1,600 in three months!) and a consistent stream of online traffic coming in from links on other websites.

I'd advise you to really get clear on who you are and what your message is before you do anything else. Then get some great photographs, start a blog, and write your bio and press release and announce your presence to local media, focusing on what people's most pressing problems are and how you can solve them.

I'm most proud that I'm going to be a featured speaker and singer at the East of England Well-Being Show, sharing the stage of celebs and TV presenters. Because of my 'cabbage dress' photo, the organisers chose my picture to promote the event in local magazines. I'm going to be interviewed by local radio stations, and I'm much more confident than I would have been because I know I'll be well prepared!

Barbara Fernandez, the Raw Rock Chick

FIONA'S STORY

I am Fiona Robertson and I am the Body Re-Newer. I specialise in two areas: mentoring to a profound new awareness of your unique relationship with food, and as a detox coach and running regular detox retreats in Biarritz, France. I am a holistic coach and mentor offering physical support for you to transform your body and be aware of your beliefs, conditioning and emotional relationship to the food that you eat.

I also run my seven day detox programs, which I currently take place in my retreat in Biarritz, south-west France, incorporating yoga and raw food.

Two years ago, my 'visibility' was rather poor. I struggled to get found by my prospective clients and I knew I needed to find a solution. I met and spoke to Janey Lee Grace and I knew instantly that I needed to work with her; her easy manner and relaxing way that she coached me was just what I need. She rightly suggested that I was hiding behind my two products using them as the face of the company, and she was right; for me, the thought of putting my head above the pedestal was unnerving. But with her guidance, that's just what I am doing now, as well as finding that I can use my existing skills to reach an audience an easier way.

I had contacted PR companies but that just seems a minefield and so expensive, and there were no guarantees that I would do any better. What Janey did was restructure me so I would be more visible myself. No PR company had ever suggested what Janey was now showing how to do myself.

I have been writing articles about detoxing for a few years and got some published by niche magazines. What Janey suggested was to go for a broader publication route and how to do that. I had advertised but rarely got any return for my huge outlay in the magazines.

I recognised my weakest link was talking in public about my passion and love for what I do, and I am still working on it, but I do feel I am getting more confident and have the guts to do it now.

As a direct result of Janey's course, I have created a new website so that I am not hiding behind the company names but use my own name, and I have had some up-to-date photos taken so that I can be seen. I am getting my articles in more mainstream magazines and having some interesting leads because of that. I now write more and am aware how to promote my own unique brand to them.

I have finished my new book, *PDQ Raw Dips, Dressings and Sauces for a saucy start to summer*, and I am setting off on a series of books to be published, which I am very excited about.

Other PR activities are newsletters, eBooks and free giveaways. I restructured myself as my brand, changed the name of the company and website, I have a blog that features all the articles I write, I have a web shop, more book ideas, and new photos of me doing what I do, as I believe pictures speak a thousand words.

I am so proud that I am here running my company and that I had the guts to do it, after starting it seven years ago when my boys were just babies and I had just moved to France. I had no idea how to get known or seen, and I just started writing and talking to people and loving what I did. I really enjoy helping people, and watching them radically change over the week. Their skin, their attitude and their energy improves measurably. I do my own program twice a year and I just believe with my whole heart that it is the best thing anyone can do for better health, positive attitude and to reconnect with your body.

My coaching had evolved as I have become more sensitive spiritually and I am more intuitive, and better at helping people go deeper within themselves to see what their body is telling them. We are all unique and I strongly believe that our eating habits, disorders and conditions are all leading us to personally unravel how to be in love ourselves more.

The journey is on the inside; we have all spent too long searching externally, and as we discover the benefits of a clean body, one that can communicate with us clearly, we can clean up and detox and go deeper within ourselves. Here, we discover our true essence and all of this helps us to fall in love with ourselves more and more, and not look for external pleasures such as food, other people or material items to fulfill any of our needs.

I am writing more about this angle and I am happy to say that it is being well received. I am even more confident to talk about this and promote myself in a way that I was not ready to do before.

Fiona Robertson, The Body Re-Newer

JANET'S STORY

I am a coach with a difference — making a difference. My business is helping people to use their minds to change their body — and their lives. I am an author (*Think More, Eat Less*), presenter and trainer with a passion for helping people.

I had a vision for creating a unique weight loss programme to go with my book *Think More, Eat Less* to deliver to clients. As a former business owner, I understand the value of good PR.

I did the PR and Media Skills Masterclass and realised that building brand awareness and contributing to local radio and TV whenever possible, writing articles etc. really helps. It re-motivated and inspired me to 'Keep going and don't give up!' I learned some great practical tips, but it was more that I had become disillusioned and demotivated and it got my fire going again. I then worked more on my brand image, my key message, and my individuality and uniqueness. I was lucky enough to get a slot on *Steve Wright in the Afternoon* on BBC Radio 2 – great for exposure for me and my book. I'd definitely advise others to align themselves with people that 'fit' well with their brand.

I am now running an exclusive weight loss retreat "EASY SLIM" with Champneys Health Spas. It is unlike any weight loss programme of its kind as it focuses on the single most important aspect of weight loss and the most ignored, i.e. the mind. I have also recorded a set of six audio tutorials and hypnotic tracks to go with a workbook so that people can follow the programme and re-programme themselves to change how they think and feel about food – and themselves. I am also writing a training programme for other therapists and coaches to be able to deliver the same programme, with my support. Alongside that, I have a members' website where they can meet and share ideas and I can provide ongoing resources in the form of regular new hypnotic tracks and practical information. My goal is to have over

100,000 people follow the EASY SLIM programme in the first two years and never have to diet again.

Janet Thomson

SUSIE'S STORY

My training is in natural therapy as I'm a reflexologist, hypnotherapist and reiki master. I'm the founder of 'Becoming a Mama' and 'The mama mentor'. My role is to support, guide and mentor mama on her emotional journey from fertility to birth. Our mission statement: At Becoming a Mama, we offer an holistic approach supporting emotional health and well-being for natural and assisted fertility, pregnancy and birth. We love to help mamas feel positive, confident and happy on their journey to becoming a mama.

A couple of years ago, I worked four days a week in a town centre clinic establishing my name with only local visibility i.e. website, local NCT pamper events with the occasional advertorial in their magazine if I paid for a series of adverts.

Before children, in my corporate days I worked at Coca-Cola in Kensington, so I witnessed first-hand the whole gambit of PR and the benefits it can bring. With this experience, I always knew that good PR would help my business to thrive and move to the next level. For me, it was just about timing!

I did the usual; invested in a good website, spoke to the local NCT for advertorials, advertised online etc. But when I left the town centre-based clinic after seven years, I decided I needed professional help to reach a wider audience.

I've attended numerous training courses, but never for PR! The best training I have ever taken part in was Janey Lee Grace's Masterclass series for Holistic Business Success. I initially had a visionary one-to-one hour call with Janey, which lead to me joining her Masterclass series.

I loved the way Janey cleverly blended and simplified the media and PR world into easy-to-follow simple steps, and the interviews with media moguls, with my favourite being Susie Pearl. The overall experience, extra bonuses and visualisation work was insightful and very cleverly thought put together giving non-media people the ability and confidence to embrace the media world with their authentic talent.

My weakest area was public speaking or, as Janey would put it, "Standing in your spotlight." Module 3 was very clever; it guided and supported me just as a parent would gently steer their nervous child to safety. As a result of the coaching, I rebranded my website, revamped my business model and realised my potential by doing my 'duty'.

Since then, I have been networking with journalists, editors of online magazines, with market leaders for fertility, pregnancy and birth, I've rebranded my website, Twitter and Faecbook business pages, and for the future I aim to share the success of the Hertfordshire Fertility Support Group.

The most successful part of the whole course were the media leads from Janey for online go-to experts for tips/advice for potential articles. The results were excellent; I appeared in *Mother & Baby* magazine online (over three months), *Take a Break* magazine (main feature), I featured as the 'go-to' expert for *Ask a Mum*, *Beauty Magazine*, Gurgle.com and *Hertfordshire Life* magazine.

I'm at the stage where I have connected to market industry journalists, and gained strong links with two fertility journalists. Above all, I've found great fulfillment doing the work I'm doing.

Susie Gower

BEV'S STORY

I am an Angel Therapy® Practitioner, Medium and Pilates expert. I am the Author of *Relax & Do Your ABC, Angelic Meaning Cards, ABC Angelic Lifestyle CD, ABC Angels CD for Children* & the *1-17 minute lazy Pilates workout MP3*. I have an absolute love of the angels, lifestyle and Pilates, and it's wonderful to pass this on to others.

I invited Janey to one of my Angel Card workshops, which was subsequently featured in *Spirit and Destiny Magazine*. Janey wrote a three-page spread for the magazine about what it's like attending a workshop.

I had several one-to-one sessions with Janey. Prior to recording my CD for children *ABC Angels*, I had some coaching of how to speak clearly on the CD to make it sound as great as possible and the speed of the delivery; this made a brilliant difference and a recording to be proud of and which children love and fall asleep to (a very different style to my CD for adults, *ABC Angelic Lifestyle*, which is deeply relaxing).

Having a one-to-one for my book *Relax & Do your ABC* was life-changing. An essential thing for me was to become an author, from the Masterclass series. I realised that by becoming an author, I would be seen as "an authority" in my work. I had been writing my book for years without clear direction, but within one hour, I had my back cover of my book clearly detailed and the whole plan for the book. So all I had to do then was focus and get it done, creating a book people can be inspired by during both the good, challenging and sad times of life.

The course was inspiring, completely enlightening as to how to do good PR. A one-hour appointment on the telephone about my book could save another wasted few years of "writing my book". I also met many gorgeous, like-minded people who share a common interest in our work.

Prior to working to Janey, I hadn't done any PR whatsoever for my Angelic Lifestyle work. I was weak when speaking about my business, but since Janey's workshop, I started a video blog and became confident quickly. Initially when I did a short presentation at the holistic business success course, I was reading from a piece of paper (not good). I am now extremely confident giving a talk as a paid speaker without any notes. A complete transformation!

I published my book *Relax & Do your ABC*. I became a regular expert in *Spirit and Destiny Magazine* writing the Q&A for readers as an Angel Therapy® Practitioner and Medium. I created my *ABC Angels CD* for children, which along with the *1-17 minute lazy Pilates workout* has been featured in *Hertfordshire Life Magazine*.

I saw incredible results, so if you're writing a book, definitely book Janey for a one-to-one or VIP day. The VIP days are extremely powerful and worth the financial investment. Janey knows her stuff, doesn't faff around, and gets on with the inspiring job in hand! It was amazing to find out your very own personal business style, which is actually of paramount business importance to know how best you can spread the word and help the most people in your work. Interestingly, I found out that I don't have just one USP; I help people who are stressed, happy, sad, going through the loss of a loved one or loved pet, entrepreneurs with no work/life balance, as well as people who love the angels and want to develop their skills from beginners to advanced level.

I am most proud that I am following my passions and dreams in my life. This has led me to many inspiration projects, allowing me to blow my own trumpet in my work, something that was worth talking and writing about in the press. Now I know that my business can go global, and without all of this professional coaching and help, I wouldn't have progressed so fast.

Producing my CD *ABC Angelic Lifestyle* was a very special moment. Writing my children's CD with my son Sammy was another breakthrough; very rewarding to see what a difference it makes in children's lives. To finally have my own deck of Angel Cards was a truly magical moment.

To become one of the experts in *Spirit and Destiny Magazine* is an honour and one I'm very proud of. To be acknowledged alongside top worldwide authors is great and can now only go from strength to strength. I am now a paid speaker and have enormous confidence in my ability to teach and inspire in my work which I didn't have at all when I started.

Bev Densham

SOPHIA'S STORY

I am a Holistic Therapist, Author & Founder of 'LT Therapy', an advanced treatment that resets muscle memory in the neck, shoulders and back, releasing emotional stress that creates physical pain in the muscle.

In terms of visibility, I was limited to my clients in my clinic in Bradford, West Yorkshire. I only built my brand on 'word of mouth' recommendations.

I needed to grow my business as I believed I had a great brand, but not the PR skills to take it to the next level.

I knew that anyone who had a successful brand used PR, so I had to do the same, or tread water.

I started to look at various PR companies on Google, but they could not relate to my industry. Then I saw what Janey Lee Grace was offering and I thought, "Yes, that's for me. She ticks all the boxes and really understands my industry due to her background in the media and association with natural products/therapies."

I found it all helpful. When you come from zero in your knowledge of PR skills to what the PR Masterclass offered, I relished every ounce of information I received. I particularly loved that I could retain all the lessons so I could go back and refresh whenever I needed too.

First, I had a one-hour consultation on the phone and knew from the moment I connected with Janey that she got me and my brand. I wanted more and the Masterclass was the ideal platform to enrol on. I loved how informative it was with lots of nuggets of information only an expert like Janey could offer, such as the 'live' interviews and how you could participate in a Q&A at the end. The whole Masterclass allowed my confidence to grow in a field I knew nothing about.

Pushing myself to take the next step was a key area of weakness for me. For so long, I had been dancing around the idea of the need to grow my brand, but an inner fear to take the next step was stopping me. I feel I have overcome that weakness now as my current success reflects that.

I wrote and published my first book within 10 months of completing the course. Something I had dreamed of doing for the past 15 years. I opened my second clinic in Harley Street, London allowing my brand to reach a wider audience. I established my brand with a new website and new business cards that truly reflected what it represented and got clarity on my target audience.

I contacted various local and national journalists for complimentary treatments to review my work and feature me in their publications.

I become more proactive on social media, building my Facebook, LinkedIn and Twitter followers. I conducted talks both locally and nationally to promote my brand, and started getting involved with key charities that my work could help.

I learned how to understand who my niche audience was. In Janey's Masterclass, she stressed that if the public know and like you, they will choose your brand. It's so easy to say your brand is for everyone, but really you have a targeted audience and in order to reach them successfully, you need to know who they are. For me, my audience are the people who suffer from ongoing neck, back and shoulder pain, but find conventional methods don't work, so what's the alternative? 'LT Therapy.'

As soon as I connected with my audience, I saw my trade treble, no longer relying on word of mouth. Social media and my new revised website was attracting the people who needed my treatment the most.

Whether you are new to the business world or as established, with over 25 years in the industry like me, there's always room for growth. PR offers a great opportunity to put your brand in the right place with the right people, but you need to invest in the right PR that understands you. For a small investment, I got a huge life transforming result as I now enjoy the fruits of my investment. Don't be frightened to grow; make sure you know your product inside out, then engage in someone who understands PR like Janey Lee Grace, who can take your brand to where you want it to be.

I am proud of developing my own treatment over 20 years that has been successfully received and accredited by the CThA, but my crowning glory has to be becoming an author. It was a dream come true and really does attract more attention raising your brand's profile to a higher level. I can now say I am an author; journalists are happy to accept my offer of a complimentary treatment in exchange for a review of my work and book in their newspaper, magazine or online. This kind of coverage is priceless.

I am living my business dream as a respected industry expert and will shortly be featured in over 22 national newspapers and magazines, thanks to working with Janey Lee Grace. Before, I lacked confidence in the area of PR. She empowered me to face the spotlight and engage with the media in order to bring the national and international success I wanted for my brand. Last November, I was invited to speak at the International Medical Conference held in Turkey and address 60 countries from around the world about my work using 'LT Therapy', something I would have declined before working with Janey. Instead, I embraced the opportunity and successfully met representatives from Dubai who are now considering working with me to train their therapists in 'LT Therapy' in their luxury spas. This has truly been my groundbreaking year and my second book, D*esperately seeking a pain-free self*, has just been published.

Sophia Kupse, The Muscle Whisperer

RECOMMENDED READING

- *Whatever You Think, Think the Opposite* by Paul Arden (Penguin)
- *Like A Virgin: Secrets They Won't Teach You at Business School* by Sir Richard Branson (Virgin Books)
- *The Ultimate Small Business Marketing Book* by Dee Blick (Filament Publishing)
- *Build Your Business in 90 minutes a Day* by Nigel Botterill and Martin Gladdish (Capstone)
- *Branding For Dummies* by Bill Chiaravalle (John Wiley & Sons)
- *The 4-Hour Work Week: Escape the 9-5, Live Anywhere and Join the New Rich* by Timothy Ferriss (Vermillion)
- *Talk Like TED: The 9 Public Speaking Secrets of the World's Top Minds* by Carmine Gallo (Macmillan)
- *Change Your Words, Change Your World* by Andrea Gardner (Hay House)
- *10 Mindful Minutes: A journal* by Goldie Hawn (Piatkus)
- *Feel The Fear And Do It Anyway* by Susan Jeffers (Vermillion)
- *Instant Confidence* by Paul McKenna (Bantam Press)
- *Speak: So Your Audience Will Listen - 7 Steps to Confident and Successful Public Speaking* by Robin Kermde (Pendle Publishing)
- *Business For Authors. How To Be An Author Entrepreneur* by Joanna Penn

- *Entrepreneur Revolution: How to develop your entrepreneurial mindset and start a business that works* by Daniel Priestley (Capstone)
- *Do Less Get More: How to Work Smart and Live Life Your Way* by Shaa Wasmund (Penguin)
- *Stop Talking, Start Doing: A Kick in the Pants in Six Parts* by Shaa Wasmund (Wiley)

ACKNOWLEDGEMENTS

A huge thanks to everyone who has supported me on my journey in PR and Media relations, everyone who has inspired me, encouraged me and offered wisdom, clarity, coffee and copious amounts of chocolate, those who have given me space to write in their homes (when my own office is just too chaotic), and those clients I have worked with who have provided such amazing feedback and valuable insights into the importance of having real clarity on your passion and purpose

Ya'll know who you are but in no particular order – and apologies in advance for anyone left out – thank you and big hugs to –

Chris Day and all at Filament Publishing, all at Hay House Publishing, Nick Williams, Shaa Wassmund, Karen Knowler, Jessica Morrrod, Helena Horlick, Kelly Dunsworth, Laura Morrison, Jo Wilson and Andy Coley, Bernado Mayo, and Louise Dockery.

Last but not least, my long suffering-family, Sonny, Buddy, Rocky and Lulu, and, of course, my ever supportive 'wind beneath' and all that... hubby Simon – none of it would have happened without your support and dedication.

Register for your free bonus gift –

Audio Masterclass module 'You are the Brand' (worth £97)

http://www.janeyleegrace.com/book-offer

Lightning Source UK Ltd.
Milton Keynes UK
UKOW06f0726271015

261457UK00002B/83/P